From J. G. Ballard, author of
Brigid Marlin:

I've finished your book—it's ⸻ ⸺⸺ ⸺⸺⸺ ⸺⸺⸻ and most impressive—a remarkable piece of work. It's a story of enormous courage on your part, extremely frank and powerfully described.

The character of Danny comes over most touchingly and grippingly. In a strange way it reminds me of *Empire of the Sun*. Like my book it is one agonized surge; one holds one's breath waiting for what's going to happen.

As a record of your own struggle as a mother, wife, painter and spiritual novice, it's most affecting. It's well-written, too, in a pacy way.

It's a remarkable other side to the painter Brigid Marlin, that cheerful, bouncy and (I think) happy woman.

From Mary Craig, author of Blessings:

Over the years, many books have been written about the problems of bringing up children with handicaps, but this one by Brigid Marlin offers an extra dimension.

Although she is a creative artist of considerable power and perceptiveness, somehow art had failed to satisfy Brigid's hunger for meaing. Only through deep personal anguish did she begin to discover her own spiritual depths and embark on a painful journey towards self-knowledge and an acceptance of her situation.

Along the way, she had to abandon her illusions and reach out for that healing compassion which is nothing more or less than an openness to the world as it really is.

From Iain Sinclair, author of Ghosts of Future London:

Brigid Marlin is an artist of conspicuous integrity. She confronts difficulty and pain with the courage of a person with a special understanding of those hallucinatory worlds within worlds—the miraculous reality of the fantastic. She understands all too well how, in the end, we become the story and how the story tells us. The duty to write, at pace, to keep up with these promptings, is always honored.

A Meaning for Danny

My Son With Asperger's Syndrome

By

Brigid Marlin

With an Epilogue by Greg Scott

Copyright © 2011 by Brigid Marlin
Cover art by Brigid Marlin

ISBN 0-7414-6692-9

Printed in the United States of America

Published October 2011

Boissevain
Books

INFINITY PUBLISHING
1094 New DeHaven Street, Suite 100
West Conshohocken, PA 19428-2713
Toll-free (877) BUY BOOK
Local Phone (610) 941-9999
Fax (610) 941-9959
Info@buybooksontheweb.com
www.buybooksontheweb.com

Contents

Part I: Life Before Danny

Part II: Danny's Life

Part III: Life After Danny

Epilogue

Foreword

This story, though it is about my son Danny, begins with my own childhood, because I have been struck to find how often early events cast their shadows forward.

Because of my extreme short-sightedness, I lived as a child in a meaningless world until I was eight years old. When later Danny's illness emerged[1] I felt thrust back again into that world of confusion and despair.

It was a long, slow fight to find hope and stability again and to make sense of the suffering that had been forced upon me.

When the unbearable happens, and still has to be borne, one comes to the end of one's resources. I went to a priest friend for help and he said, "God did not promise that we would not suffer, but He did promise that we would not suffer alone. He is always with you if you turn to Him."

From that moment when things got bad I would withdraw for a bit and say to God, "I can't bear this; please bear it for me!"

Always I got enough support to carry on. Sometimes only enough for one more step, and sometimes so much inner peace and help that I could say with St. Augustine, "Not I that live, but Thou that livest in me."

---

[1] The term "Asperger's syndrome" was unknown at the time I first started writing this book; I only discovered it later, when I met Greg Scott, who has kindly written the Epilogue to this book which provides a brief introduction to Autism and Autism Spectrum Disorders. I have also changed various names, to give people privacy.

Part I

Life Before Danny

Chapter One

Beginnings

"Look at that heartless child!" my mother said. I was three years old, and I had been crayoning next to Mother until she got up and walked into the mist on the other side of the room. Then the mist had suddenly turned into blazing orange light, very beautiful. Mother had screamed, and I heard my father run in and soon the bright light went out. Mother went on, "I could have died in the fire and she just sat there and watched!"

I didn't understand, but I felt deeply guilty, knowing I must have done something wrong. It was always happening to me. Although I was in a secure and loving home with parents, a grandmother and an older sister and younger brother, I was beginning to realize that in some mysterious way I was different from other children, and I lived in fear of being found out.

But there were memories of joy too. That early time when I had pushed open the screen door at the back of the kitchen and escaped, feeling the grooves of the wooden floor of the porch scratchy against my bare feet. I climbed carefully down the wide porch steps to where a blank mist of green faced me. I stepped towards it and then to my surprise I brushed against a plant with blue flowers higher than my head. I reached out for a flower the size of my hand and peered into it.

It sparkled in the early morning light. Its center was a soft turquoise, the outer petals a deeper blue. As I gazed, the blueness seemed to expand. Waves of blue engulfed me, and I felt drawn into the heart of the flower. I stood in rapture till Mother found me and carried me in to breakfast.

Inside the house there was always a brown mist, but when the light poured in through the window, I could see tiny specks of dust shining near my eyes.

My older sister Olga could go out the front door on to the street. When she went out one day and brought back another little girl, a neighbor's child, I felt betrayed.

When I tried to go out the front door like Olga there was a gray mist, and when I walked further there was a loud hooting noise and strange people shouted at me.

So instead I used to go to the back garden, where I peered at the ground and saw the flowers. I loved to thread the dandelions into wreaths and blow on the gauzy dandelion clocks. I wondered at what point the life of the dandelion began. I looked in the grass for smaller and smaller green buds and on opening them I found tiny new dandelions getting ready to be born, but no matter how I searched I could never find the exact moment when the bud itself came into being, and I wondered where its life came from.

When I was four years old a new baby sister, Sheila, was born. Olga was five and deserted me to help Mother with her. Now my younger brother Randal and I were thrown together. He wanted to play trains and I wanted to play mummies and daddies. He said if I played trains today, tomorrow he would play my game. But when the next day came he wouldn't play mummies and daddies.

"It isn't tomorrow now, it's today!" he said.

In her room upstairs, away from the bustle of the house, Granny read stories to us. I loved fairy tales about witches and princesses best; Randal liked adventure stories. But we both loved the story of the twins who were marooned on an iceberg with a polar bear. He chased them round and round the edge until they escaped in a raft.

Randal and I decided to be marooned. We said that an Oriental rug on the blue carpet was our raft, and the blue carpet was the sea. But we had to save Granny, who was comfortably reading in the middle of the sea. At last she understood her peril and moved on to the rug with us. Just in time!

That summer we went to the country, to a place called Lake Champlain. There we lived in a house with a mysterious big garden. I was sure there would be fairies living in this garden. I mixed a drink of sugar and water and left it out for the Fairy Queen to change overnight into a magic potion. Olga scoffed at me. She was not interested in fairies. In the morning I hurried down and out into the porch where without looking I took a great gulp of my magic potion.

My world came to an end. I was seized with a black horror. Ants were walking down my throat, swarming around my tongue, going in and out of my teeth. There were millions of them. I ran around in circles screaming, with my tongue hanging out.

This was the worst moment of my life. I thought I was going to die. Our jolly maid came out and scraped my tongue with a kindly brown finger. She sat me down and gave me a glass of water and told me not to cry, Honey.

I drank the water. I thought of all the live ants in my stomach, and I was not sure I would live. But Olga, who had been watching me with interest, told me that they would now be drowned. I drank some more water just to make sure.

Soon after that Granny went away visiting. I felt lost without her. Mother was so busy always. I was following Olga down the path to the lake. We were wearing the swimming suits Granny knitted for us. They were very disagreeable, soggy when damp, and riding up uncomfortably inside our buttocks, but Granny was so proud of having made them that we never complained.

Then I heard Mother calling out that our grandmother was here on a visit. I ran back, arms outstretched, towards the shadowy bulky form of my much-loved Granny.

She bent her face close to mine and I screamed in horror. A witch had changed Granny's face! Her snow-white hair had become iron gray. Her beautiful pale face had become broad and red. Her gray eyes were now the color of mud. Her silvery voice had become hoarse as she pushed me away, saying, "Get away, you silly child!"

Later I found out my mistake. I hadn't realized that people had two grandmothers. But after that unfortunate beginning my other grandma never really took to me.

Back at home Mother used to go to a room upstairs that she called her Studio. When you stood next to the walls you could touch lots of paintings there, stacked against the wall. The oil paint smelled rich and musty. Mother held a brown wooden thing which she called a palette; when I peered at it I could see lots of colored paint on it in heaps like bright little mountains.

One day Mother was painting my portrait. She told me to sit near her in the chair. She had a large white canvas in front of her. There were lots of brushes in a jar near her. She took a brush out and hit the canvas. Then she leaned back. Then she leaned forward and took another brush. She kept hitting the canvas as if she was angry with it. After awhile my legs ached from dangling down from the hard chair. I wanted to go out. Mother told me I had to keep sitting there. Olga and Randal banged at the door, wanting to come in. Mother shouted at them to go away.

She got more and more angry at the canvas and hit it harder and harder. I whined to be let out so Mother started to tell me a story about a witch. Every now and then she stuck a brush in her mouth so I couldn't hear the story very well. While she was telling it she kept on looking at the canvas and hitting it. I was sick of sitting still, and the smell of the oil paint and turpentine was overpowering.

At last I sighed and said, "I don't want to be a mother."

"Why not?" asked my mother.

"I don't want to have to paint pictures all the time."

Mother laughed and told this to Granny. They often spoke in a language we children couldn't understand, which was Dutch.

In spite of my remark to Mother I did love to paint and draw. Bending close over my drawing I could see clearly to put in all the details I loved, but when I looked further off everything was blurred. But I could see sparkles from shiny things. A candle flame always had a halo of tiny sparkling lines surrounding it, amazingly beautiful.

One afternoon Olga and I were playing in Mother's room. I was poking into Mother's big sewing box when I pulled out a little rubber doll. Looking at it I received a jolt. I felt dizzy with a rushing sensation as though I were being pulled back through time—telescoped back to a primitive era. It was very strange.

"What is this?" I asked Mother, holding out the doll. She laughed and said, "Oh! How funny! That was a doll you were very fond of when you were a baby!"

One day when I was four and a half years old Granny took me by the hand and led me to a strange place. She called it kindergarten. It was a big dark room in a place I didn't know. It was full of strangers. Then Granny was gone. I was filled with total despair. I didn't know why I was left in this place, it didn't make any sense. I thought Granny was my friend, I thought she loved me, and now she had abandoned me. I couldn't stop crying. Everything looked blurred and dark gray like a prison. I felt as though the darkness was closing round me and I was falling down a deep hole. I couldn't understand what was happening or why I was there.

Someone put a dirty toy rabbit in my hands. It smelled like garbage and I hated it. There was a lady like a witch with a black cape. She said her name was Sistertarsissius. She said to the children: "Brigid won't stop crying, so I want you to laugh at her, everybody laugh."

It was like the moment in Alice in Wonderland when all the cards rise up to attack Alice. It was the final horror.

A few years later when I got to know Sister Tarsissius better she ceased to be a monster to me, and I saw that she was a small practical nun with little imagination. I am convinced she never realized what effect her words would have on my life.

Once a child is made an object of derision to the other children, their attitude does not change. Their laughter against me continued for the next six years of my life there at the school.

It was only many years later that I could look back and accept that painful experience. Because of what was going to happen in my life I was going to need to know what it felt like to be in despair and cut off from others.

Chapter Two

School

When it came time to go to first grade, Olga led me there by the hand, and only gradually did I learn to grope my way there and back by myself. In grade school we sat in desks, in rows. Next to me was a little boy with a very white face covered in pale freckles. He held his shaking hands in front of him like a squirrel and made funny animal noises. When the teacher handed out crayons and paper with a drawing on it to color, he seized a black crayon and scribbled all over the page.

The teacher was angry with him and shouted. I was amazed. In our house we made colored pictures all the time. It was fun, and we children could draw in whatever color we liked. I had never thought it was something you could be scolded for.

The little boy looked more unhappy than ever and wrung his shaking hands together. I never saw him again after that day, but I remembered him clearly, because his bewilderment seemed to express what I was feeling.

Then I made a friend, a little boy called Michael, who sat behind me. We were going to marry and live in a tree house when we grew up. Whenever I felt unhappy, I could turn around and see Michael's blurred face and he would smile at me.

But one day after the summer I turned around to smile at Michael and found that he had gone! Instead there was a boy with a scowling face called Howard Blackett.

It was like the time when I had looked into the face of my Granny and found her changed. I was sick with shock. Howard Blackett was pleased at my fright, and whenever he could he pulled my pigtails. Then he started waiting for me after school with a crowd of other boys, and they beat me up regularly. I took to hiding, and arrived home late every day. On the way home there was a vacant house with a deserted garden where I could sit and dream.

I lived in a mental fog as well as a visual one, because by then I had given up trying to make sense of the world, things came to me out of the mist, and vanished into the mist without any logic, though other people had the surprising ability to dart through this fog with ease.

I was always being scolded for my vagueness and clumsiness, affectionately by my family and crossly by my teachers. My fear grew that I was horribly different from other children so I did everything to conceal the truth, pretending that I was the same as the others: seeing what they saw, knowing what they knew, trying all the time to conceal the secret of my real condition, feeling that if they knew I was different I would be cast out like a leper.

I took refuge in fairy tales. There I found a world that made sense. Goodness was rewarded and evil punished. I began to withdraw from the real world to live in a magic world that I had created. I loved anything I could pick up and examine; pieces of broken glass, which I found by tracing their sparkle on the road, I collected and called them my "jewels."

One day I found a piece of glass that had broken in such a way that it produced a rainbow in certain lights; this was my greatest treasure. But after awhile I grew unhappy with it. Why could the rainbow only be seen in certain lights, under certain conditions? I wanted it to be there always.

This longing began to drive me to set down the images I loved. Now I spent all my time in painting and drawing in my wish to create something beautiful that would stay the same forever.

Apart from painting and drawing, my happy moments were away from school. Randal and I liked to go exploring. He would pedal his tricycle with me riding on the back carrying sandwiches I had made for us, and we would go on a "venture." He seemed to be able to manage the road safely, so with him I could go outside and travel to other neighborhoods and meet different children with different tribal customs. Together we experienced all the thrills of the early explorers finding the source of the Nile.

Randal was interested in places. He told me we lived

"on Northampton Avenue
in Chevy Chase
in Washington, D.C.
in America
on Earth
in the Solar System
in the Universe."

One time Father took us to see the White House, where the President lived. Randal was excited but I couldn't see anything, so Father was disappointed in my reaction.

At home Mother and Granny scolded me. They pointed out that Olga and even Randal who was younger could go shopping but I couldn't. I didn't know what or where the shops were. Olga and Randal could tell the time. Granny talked about something called a clock.

"I bet you can't even see the clock!" Olga jeered. "Of course I can!" I said quickly, wondering what a clock was.

I never knew what was going on in school, so I was treated as an idiot by the nuns and put at the back of the class. I learned nothing there, but sat and drew pictures of fairies all day in my exercise books. Luckily my grandmother was fond of teaching and from her I had learned to read and write and do sums.

At eight years old, in the confusion of a large household with yet another new baby's arrival, brother John, I was old enough to escape supervision. Retreating from the outer world I neglected my appearance, and arrived at school with unbrushed hair and rumpled clothes, becoming more than ever the object of derision. and bullying from the other children. I avenged myself by imagining that I was a fairy princess, and at any moment I could throw off my grubby school uniform and reveal a dazzling dress of diamonds to astonish them all!

Then one day everything changed for me. It seemed at first like any other day. The class was going through a weird ritual that they had often done before. The rows of children would all say numbers in turn. When it got to my turn I tried to join in and said a number, but whatever number I chose would make everyone laugh, for some reason.

In the middle of this game the bell rang for fire drill. As we filed out past the teacher's desk I saw to my surprise that the top of her desk was a white blur instead of brown. I put out my hand to see if it were snow. No, it wasn't wet and cold.

I peered over the top and saw large cards printed with sums. They were easy sums; I did much harder ones with Granny.

Waiting in the playground I was puzzled, thinking over the cards I had seen. None of the sums had answers on them. Could there be a connection between these sums and the numbers that the children had been saying? We filed back into class and a strange feeling grew in me, as if my stomach knew something that was too big for my head to hold. The number game began again, they were going down my row; it was my turn.

I stood up. The feeling in my stomach shot up through me like lightning, splitting my head in two. In that enormous flash, all the pieces fitted together at last, and I understood.

"I can't see! I can't see!" I shouted, laughing with joy because so many things were clicking into place at once; I had been blundering all my life in a fog, but other people could see clearly.

I wasn't stupid, I wasn't clumsy; I just couldn't see well. *Something was wrong with my eyes!* It was more than a solution to a mystery, it was as if light was pouring down into my head. I saw that things made sense, that there was Meaning, that there was God.

The teacher, Sister Marie, was very angry. Now I realize that if I had cried when saying I couldn't see, she might have been sympathetic, but as I was laughing she assumed that her least favorite pupil was having a joke at her expense. She said witheringly, "Of course you can see!"

"I really can't!" I said, no longer laughing. She marched down the aisle and, pinching my ear between a cold finger and thumb, yanked me to the front of the class and pushed me into a front seat. "Now you can see!" she snapped.

I saw that she was indeed holding up a card, just as I had guessed. It was a thrilling moment. This is what had been taking place all those times without my knowing! Unfortunately the card was still too blurred to read.

"I still can't see." I said apologetically, knowing it would annoy her even more. It did. She slammed the card towards my face, shouting, "*Now* can you see?" Just before it hit my nose I read the numbers 6 + 7 = ? I pushed her hand away and said, "Yes, and the answer's 13."

To my surprise she stood completely frozen, like a statue. Then she backed away as if I were a dangerous animal and said in a nervous voice: "Don't move! Stay there! I'll be back!" I heard her hurried footsteps leaving the room. In a few moments there was a lot of noise and bustle and a swirling of black veils.

My next clear memory is of sitting in a room where a man in a white coat asked me to read the letters on a chart. "What chart?" I asked.

His voice sounded amazed as he said, "Can't you even see the chart!" Neither he nor anyone seemed to be able to believe that for eight years I had lived and gone to school with so little sight.

I began to understand that it was my fear of being different that had kept me and everyone else in ignorance for so long.

Chapter Three

Glasses

At this point I became the center of a great deal of sympathy and fuss. "Why didn't you tell us you couldn't see?" said Granny and Mother reproachfully. When I mulled this over, I thought to myself that after all I didn't know I couldn't see; I might just as easily have said to them, "Why didn't you tell me you *could* see?"

But I was too happy to complain. At last that terrible fog had rolled away, and there was hope because at last I could begin to make sense of the world. It was not going to be easy, however. Accepting this new reality was difficult; I had lived too long in a misty world and it had taught me habits of isolation.

My first adjustment came on the morning when my spectacles arrived by post. Mother announced to the family, "Brigid's glasses have come! This is a wonderful moment for her. For the first time in her life she will be able to see clearly!" I could sense the whole family watching as with trembling fingers I opened the metal arms and fitted the glasses on my nose.

I looked up. Until that moment I had only seen one thing distinctly at a time, framed against a background of subtly coloured mist. Now everything rushed at me at once, clamouring for attention. I saw stains on the wall, dirt on the baby's bib, the baby's face, a teacup on the table, the buttons on my sister's dress, Mother and Granny beaming at me, the pattern on the carpet, my brother eating his corn flakes, the canary in his cage, cracks on the ceiling, the window, and though the window I saw the street, and the neighbour's house and beyond that the alley where we played and further than that a multitude of things! It was too much to cope with I burst into tears.

It was some time before my eyes could adjust to the whirling kaleidoscope of things in front of them, but over time my eyes learned the trick of selecting the thing that was important, and letting the rest stay in the background.

However, it was not just the difficulty of adjusting my eyes to the glasses, there was the even greater difficulty of adjusting myself.

Over the years, cut off in some measure from communication with the outside world, I had spun for myself an imaginary world which had become a cocoon which protected me from the teasing of the schoolchildren and the nagging of the teachers. Now my new glasses were opening up the real world to me, I felt uncomfortable. Ostrich-like, I had assumed that when I couldn't see the other children at school, they couldn't see me. Now that I saw their faces and eyes I felt threatened and vulnerable; I missed my comfortable old cocoon. I longed to escape into Fairyland and be protected from the ugliness of reality. If only I could be stolen away, like the child in Yeats's poem to whom the fairies said,

> Come away O human child,
> To the water and the wild
> With a fairie, hand in hand.
> For the world's more full of weeping
> Than you can understand.

However, no matter how often I waited at early morning or evening by a likely clump of flowers, no supernatural creature appeared to steal me away. According to Irish legends they preferred boys, anyway!

When Mother's tenth book came out she was asked by a journalist how she managed to write and paint with six children around. Mother said, "By neglecting my duties!" and it made the headlines.

My father was employed at the International Civil Aviation Organisation, a United Nations agency. Although ICAO had its base in Montreal, when surrounded by six quarrelling children and several dogs, my father discovered that he needed to fly off to warm countries to sort out their airports and pilot-training schemes.

As he had been away during the war as well, he became a rather remote figure to his children, an Olympian demigod who descended from from the skies from time to time to ask, "Have you brushed your teeth?" and, "Where are your slippers?" We children only really got to know him when we were older.

When I turned thirteen I was unwillingly dragged into adolescence. My limbs sprouted, an unwanted bosom made its appearance. I misjudged distances and banged my elbows getting through doorways. I felt like Alice in Wonderland, too big now to get through the door into the magical garden. I became morose and introverted.

One day I was crying upstairs in an outburst of temper when I heard a strange voice inside me say, "Why are you making all this fuss? It isn't important!" I sat up, startled. Where did that voice come from?

It was another indication of an inner life that I knew nothing about.

Chapter Five

Adolescence

Our family now moved to a different part of Montreal and in my new school I went back to being unpopular again, but this time I didn't care. I still wrote to Henriette, the lost Princess of my childhood, but she by this time had really grown up and didn't write back often.

So I turned to the world of books and read all the great Victorian novels, crouched under the dining room table where my brothers and sisters couldn't find me.

At school I used long words from the novels, and so was considered to be "stuck-up" by the girls. I ignored them and tried to please the teachers instead. I was good at schoolwork and art so I earned praise from them, which I basked in.

But one winter day when I had turned fourteen, I was struggling to school, my sketchbook under my arm, when a thought struck me so forcefully that I stopped in my tracks.

Somewhere a voice said to me, What if this praise were to end? I thought, Well, my family would still admire me. But then I realised that one day my parents also would be dead. Then nobody would care if I did anything well or not. This thought made me so desolate that I pushed it away.

During the week of what was to be my last term at that school, the nuns asked me and another girl, Maureen, to paint a background for a play that they were putting on. When we had finished the nuns filed in to the front rows to criticise what we had done.

times I have tried to distinguish the difference between egocentric and egotistic.

Learning to paint was an absorbing task. Oil paint was extremely difficult to handle—it slid and skidded from your brush and sank into the hardboard without a trace. I felt as if I were falling down a deep well and couldn't climb out. The oil paint was so difficult to handle and ended up like mud, whatever colours I started out with. A student then informed me that I needed to "prime" the board, otherwise the paint would keep soaking in because the board was acting like blotting paper. I learned to boil up glue size and coat the board with it before I started painting.

My mother had warned me that when I went to art school I would lose all my imagination for awhile, but that it would come back later. Her words proved true; I was to spend years at various art schools, learning disciplines and techniques, but all this time I was out of touch with my real inner vision.

When working with other young artists there was always a silent battle over whose work was going best, and I began to reflect that if I fell in love with another painter and married him, we might go on having fights over who was the better artist, so I ignored the art school dances and smuggled myself instead into the dances at Olga's college to meet boys. I became quite flirtatious, and left off my glasses as much as I could, convinced I looked prettier without them. This led to a lot of difficulties because I smiled at everyone in case I knew them, and was always having problems with men who thought I was trying to pick them up.

At seventeen I met Jim, an Irish engineer, at a Trinity College Ball. He invited me to the Engineers Ball, and while we had supper I learned that he was a Protestant.

"Oh, then we can never marry!" I said gaily. "I'm a Catholic!"

Jim said nothing but he looked annoyed. Maybe this became a challenge, because he invited me out repeatedly. I went because I loved parties, but I was determined not to have different religions in the family. Although my own parents had married in the Anglican Church and shared the same faith at first, Father had not become a Catholic when Mother did, and this was a great grief to her. I wanted my marriage to be perfect with no divisions.

However, I found Jim's company stimulating; he opened up a different world to me, a solid world. He described his father's struggles with the family business, and the interaction between all his relatives, and the whole community life of a small town in the middle of Ireland. Our family had always lived in big cities so we had never experienced the life of a community. I was also impressed by his practical knowledge of how people interact with each other.

When I was eighteen years old, one evening after a dance Jim and I sat by the sea and he told me I was everything he ever dreamed of, and he couldn't bear the thought of life without me.

It was a moonlit night, and when he stood up on the rocks with the wind ruffling his hair and spoke of the tragedy that would divide us forever he looked dreadfully lonely. Then he said that we must part and never see each other again because of the difference in our faiths. I wept over the agony of it. It seemed so terrible that poor Jim would have to live out his life without me. I knew our hearts would be broken forever!

We parted and didn't see each other for three whole months. Then we met by accident on the street, and began to go out together again. I was heartbroken to think we must eventually part, and then I remembered the old fairy tale that said if you wanted something enough you could get it.

Here at last was something I really wanted. Jim must become a Catholic. I decided to storm Heaven with my prayers and demands. For three years I gave up sweets and said three rosaries a day.

Then when I was twenty-one and the family had moved back to Montreal, Jim came out to Canada and my wish was granted. He became a Catholic and we were married on June 27th, 1957, in Montreal.

I was triumphant. To me it proved that the old saying was right: If you wanted anything enough you would get it. Without realising it, I was still believing in fairies.

Chapter Six

The Birth

From the first Jim and I had decided that we weren't going to be boring and domesticated like other young couples around us. Jim got a job with Montreal Engineering and soon acquired a shiny green MG convertible sports car and I, fresh from art school, was as convinced of my unique artistic genius as all the other young art students.

We defied convention by living in a rented ramshackle hut in the country, which I decorated with murals, including a large whale spouting water above the bath. We bought a jaunty red fridge which seemed to be a symbol of our carefree life together.

At first there were difficulties adjusting to each other. I came from a noisy argumentative family, and Jim from a soft-spoken Anglo-Irish background. When I was painting I was used to yelling at my brothers and sisters to leave me in peace, but I discovered that husbands didn't take kindly to this treatment and I learned to modify my behaviour.

I expected us to sit down and work out our finances together, so that I would learn how to manage money. But Jim said, "Don't worry your pretty head about things like that. I'll do it all." I was pleased with the compliment and felt looked-after and safe.

It was a shock when I found that I was pregnant. Jim and I didn't quite believe it. We made jokes about having babies, and thought that we'd move to the Yukon so I could give birth on an ice floe and make history, but in the event I developed toxemia and had to go early into the hospital.

On April 29, 1958, the baby was induced. The birth was quick; through the anaesthetic I felt a cut, then a slippery, slithering sensation as the baby came out. The doctor held him up, saying, "It's a fine boy!"

When I heard his first cry, I thought, "So this is it. Now I am a Mother!" There was a feeling of exhilaration and love but also the depressing thought that from now on my life would change. I would have to be responsible for this child for the next twenty-one years.

As I wasn't wearing my glasses I only saw a blur, but when they placed him in my arms I saw a small red face, which looked as if it had been pushed into life too soon.

Jim came into the room soon after I'd been moved there, and held the baby very carefully in his hands. "You look as though you've been hit on the head with a large hammer!" I said.

"Yes," he said slowly, "I suppose it is a big shock, having a son." He jiggled the baby gently on his lap. "We'll call him Daniel, after my father." (Jim's father had died earlier.)

I had a private room in the hospital because I was planning to breast-feed the baby myself. At that time bottle-feeding was in fashion so I was regarded as an eccentric. The nurses came to warn me solemnly never to fall asleep with the baby in my bed, so after each feeding and changing I kept nervously putting him back in the little plastic box they had given me for a cradle.

Danny was not a happy child. He cried all the time. One night, exhausted by his constant crying, I fell asleep with him in my arms. It was the only time he didn't cry all night, but I was too frightened of the nurses to let it happen again.

After a week the baby and I were allowed to leave and Jim came to drive us home to the rickety wooden house which we had rented. The baby's room was ready with a bassinet tied up with ribbons and flowers painted on the green floor. My mother came for a few days to help with the baby, and then I was on my own.

The baby continued to cry, night and day. I read in Dr. Spock's book of baby care that it was fine to let babies cry once you've checked that there was nothing wrong with them. But Danny was very strong physically. If he were left crying for any length of time he would manage to wedge himself in his bassinet or pram in some painful way, so I never could be sure he was safe to leave even for a moment.

The one time Danny would stop crying was when he was being driven in the car. So we gave up sailing and on weekends and holidays we loaded the carrycot into the back space of the MG sports car and drove for miles. It was perfect peace until we had to stop and get out. I learned to breast feed and change the nappy as we drove so we could go for a long time without stopping.

Gradually the crying stopped. As Danny began to crawl and explore the world, we bought him a swing and a walker.

When Danny was eight months old I began to feel incredibly tired. I went to the doctor and was informed that I was pregnant again. I was very surprised as my mother had told me that you couldn't become pregnant while you were nursing.

"An old wives' tale!" sniffed the doctor. So it appeared.

One Saturday morning I was sleeping late, Danny was cruising around me in his walker. I had left the bedroom door open to get some heat from the wood stove below; the Canadian winters were bitterly cold. I had set up a barrier across the doorway that Danny couldn't cross, but I hadn't realised that what a child cannot do one day he can suddenly do the next.

Danny heard the voice of his father talking to a friend downstairs and wanted to go to him. He climbed out of his walker and over the barrier and crawled to the stairs where he fell, rolling from step to step to the bottom.

I was woken by Jim's angry voice. I leapt out of bed aghast and raced downstairs. Danny lay white and still in his father's arms, but he was still breathing.

I took the baby from him with trembling hands, praying, "Oh God! Let him be all right!" His face was deathly pale. Jim rang the doctor while I rocked Danny gently, holding him in my arms. At last his eyelids fluttered. Then I thought of nursing him. He began to suckle and gradually the colour returned to his cheeks. By the time the doctor arrived, tramping through the snow, Danny was laughing and looking embarrassingly healthy.

The doctor examined the baby closely and Danny was fine, he hadn't even a bruise as he was all bundled up in winter woollies; he had been suffering from shock.

But I felt terribly guilty about his fall, as it had been caused by my laziness, and later I was to wonder if there had been some damage after all.

Certainly Danny did not show any ill effects after the fall, except for one thing he became timid about walking. He would not now go anywhere by himself unless he could hold on to something, a wall or a table. Gradually I weaned Danny; he never would take a bottle but went straight on to ordinary food. Even so, I worried about leaving him to go to the hospital to have the second baby. Danny seemed so dependent on me, and so vulnerable.

My parents invited us to visit them in their country house in the Laurentian mountains. It was wonderful to go there and be looked after. By now I was eight months pregnant. My mother put me on a diet with raw vegetables and fruit, only allowing me potatoes and bread to stay the pangs of hunger.

Except for Olga, my brothers and sisters were all there on vacation. Sheila was a very pretty art student; she and Mother and I made sketches of Danny. Liz, a clever, energetic schoolgirl, took him for little walks. John and Randal, back from college and boarding school, clowned around together and enjoyed talking to Jim when he came up for weekends.

Danny took a long time to get used to the new place. He didn't seem to like change. He made little complaining noises at the feel of grass under his bare feet, and seemed lost without his familiar surroundings. Mother discovered that Danny loved rhythm, and amused him for long stretches of time by tapping on the wooden arm of her deck chair with her fingers.

My father was delighted to be a grandfather, but to his chagrin he found that Danny was frightened of him. He bought several new toys that made noises of various kinds, but Danny was frightened of them too.

One day my father, who had always been ambitious for us all to succeed, asked me, "Why doesn't Danny talk?" I hadn't thought about it before but then I realised that Danny at a year and three months was a little late in talking. However, he had developed into a good-looking child with long-lashed blue eyes under a mop of soft gold curls, and he had begun to lose his timidity and walked well with a very straight body.

At the end of the summer, just before I was due to go into the hospital in Montreal, the second baby was born suddenly in the country. Liz had to bicycle to the nearest village to get the doctor to deliver it. Liz saw the baby being born, and perhaps it was then that her interest in medicine began.

This baby looked like a wise old man, and we named him Charles. We made a cradle from a bureau drawer and dressed him in one of Danny's vests, which fell off his tiny shoulders.

In the morning I called Danny to see his new brother, but he was not very interested. Instinctively I avoided nursing Charlie in front of Danny, feeling it might upset him. It was easy to hide this from him as Danny lived in his own world. He went around humming to himself, a dreamy look in his eyes. I had just read a story about the early life of Beethoven, who acted like this as a child, so I decided Danny must be a genius and waited eagerly to see what talents he would develop.

Part II

Danny's Life

Chapter Seven

London

Jim and I dreaded another Canadian winter, so one day after a long discussion we decided to go to live in England. Jim wanted to get another degree at the London School of Economics. He could work during the day and go to evening classes.

I imagined that London, being one of the centres of the art world, would launch my painting career. Another advantage was that we could invite Jim's mother in Ireland to live with us, as she had been left very poor after her husband had died.

So Jim flew to London to arrange things. He found a job with an engineering company, and his old school friend, Shane, found him a flat near his own digs. When Charlie was six weeks old I flew to London with Sheila, who was returning to the art school in Amsterdam and could help me with the babies.

Jim, his mother and Shane met us. Jim's mother was a thin Irish woman with a whimsical sense of humour. She became known as "Gran" right away.

In the few days that Sheila stayed with us, Shane was very struck with her. Jim and I noticed this and wondered if anything might come of it. We invited Sheila to visit us from Holland, to give the romance a chance.

Gran and I soon became fast friends, so much so that one day she confided to me that she had been very hurt when Jim changed his religion. I blushed when she told me this, and confessed that I had given up sweets for three years so that Jim would be converted.

"That wasn't fair!" she said. "If I'd known you were doing that I'd have given up something too!" She thought for a moment and added, "Well, I don't eat too many sweets, so it would have had to be something else, maybe meat." Suddenly we both saw the funny side and began to laugh.

Gran was very popular with the children. The baby chuckled and grinned when she held him and Danny, after an initial shyness, completely adored her. She loved telling him stories and singing him little songs which Danny would croon over to himself afterwards.

He had a funny way of enjoying himself; one of his pleasures was pulling his father's ties down from the tie-rack. He could just reach the ends of them and he did this whenever we forgot and left the wardrobe door open. Another of his pleasures was to stick his little fist in the jam jar and lick up jam whenever we weren't looking.

One day when Gran was baby-sitting we came back and Gran greeted us saying, "Danny has been wonderful, he hasn't made a sound all morning!" Jim and I both groaned simultaneously and rushed through the flat to our back bedroom. Danny was sitting blissfully under the tie-rack. He had carried a pot of marmalade into the bedroom and was alternately scooping up a mouthful of marmalade and pulling down a tie. Every one was covered in sticky goo.

One day, when Charlie was about four months old, Danny suddenly came upon me breast-feeding him. His face went white with shock and he flung himself full-length on the floor in a faint. I hurriedly put Charlie in his cot and ran to pick up Danny. I sat him on my lap and rocked him like an infant. Gradually he opened his eyes; then I saw the baby's half-finished bowl of cereal on the table. I took the spoon and gently began to feed Danny, murmuring over and over, "Mummy loves you too, Danny."

He began to suck the spoon, and slowly the colour returned to his cheeks. I walked around the room with him in my arms, singing to him, then I brought him to his cot and tucked him into bed.

Danny gave me a beaming smile, closed his eyes and fell asleep. I turned to pick up Charlie, who had been waiting patiently all this time. I was trembling and my hands were shaking. I felt as if some dreadful crisis had been narrowly averted.

After a few more months Gran obtained a live-in job. She had enjoyed her stay with us but now she wanted to be independent. We all missed her, especially Danny, who wandered around like a lost soul, his playmate gone.

Two weeks later Gran had a weekend off and came to see us. She stretched out her arms to Danny but he wouldn't go near her. She was surprised and hurt. "I suppose he must have forgotten me already!" she said. I was getting dinner ready when I heard Gran cry out, "What is it, Danny? Why are you looking at me like that?" I went to the sitting room to see what was the matter and Gran said, "Danny keeps looking at me with such hurt eyes! He makes me feel as if I've betrayed him by going away!" Gran tried to take Danny out for a walk as she used to do, but he wouldn't go. Gran was very upset, but no one could change Danny's attitude.

When Gran went back to work again I began to feel trapped and depressed. In Canada we had never had any real money worries, Jim's salary had been good, and I had felt that my parents were always there in the background as security.

But in England Jim's salary was very much less, just enough for us all to live on. London was still suffering the after-effects of the war. There were bomb sites around, and due to the pollution from the coal fires burning in every home the air was grimy and the houses and streets looked dirty. On foggy days you could see the famous London smog, a mixture of fog and smoke. However, the artistic effect was splendid; the sky was an opaque gold with figures and buildings seen through it all blurred and magical.

I longed to paint it, but there was so much work to get through every day that there didn't seem to be any time.

To do the shopping I carried the baby and walked the toddler down four flights of stairs; there was no elevator, or "lift" as they called it here. Then we had to cross the large car-park until we reached a lockup shed at the back where the pram was kept. The door was unlocked, the pram taken out, the door relocked and both boys put into the large nanny-like pram. Then we went to queue in turn at the four or five different shops to get the food needed for dinner.

The big problem came after we got back to the shed and I was left with two baby boys and a large bag of shopping. You couldn't trust Danny not to run into the road if he weren't held; if I locked the baby into the shed and took Danny and the shopping back first, when I went back to get the baby, Danny would eat the groceries. It was the fox, the goose and the bag of grain.

I didn't seem to be able to find friends. In America and Canada people smiled at you and said "Hi!" Here they drew together in clusters and muttered as I came in to collect the family allowance money. When they heard my American accent I heard them saying indignantly, "They come over here and take jobs from our boys!" It was exactly what we'd heard the Canadians say of the English and Irish in Canada.

Along with the family allowance I also collected a strange bottle of condensed orange juice that tasted of mushrooms. This was for the children, but they didn't seem to like it much, nor the brown bottle of malt extract, and they didn't like the free cod-liver oil at all. I asked why we were getting these and Jim explained that an English government minister, Sir Stafford Cripps, had organised these supplements to the diet of British children because of the need for rationing, and because of this the children were healthier in wartime than ever before.

There was still a feeling of scarcity, although it was 1959 and rationing had ended a few years before. I missed the free and easy life we'd had in Montreal and the beauty of the Canadian countryside. We lived in an unattractive part of London called Cricklewood, though it did boast a little crooked shop with wooden beams which had a sign saying "Founded in 1492." I gazed at it in awe—that was the year that Columbus discovered America!

Inside the shop there was a little crooked old man to match. When I first went in he smiled at Danny and offered him a sweet. Danny was delighted, but when we went in next he expected the same thing to happen and whined for a sweet. The old man frowned and said that Danny was greedy. I was upset, I knew it wasn't greed, it was just that he lived by ritual. So after that I kept sweets in my pocket ready to give Danny if we needed to go in there.

There were so many differences that I found it hard to adjust to. The money was another problem. There were two large silver coins very similar, the half crown and the florin. Because I had an American accent, I was always being cheated and given the smaller value coin for the larger. At last I got angry and resolved to make a stand. In the bakery shop I received a florin when I was expecting a half crown. I protested, and the woman behind the counter made a huge fuss, calling upon all the other customers to support her. I was sure then that I'd made a mistake and turned to flee, grabbing my son's hand. To complete my shame, Danny had wet himself and stood in a pool. I never dared to go into that shop again.

Now with very little money and no friends I felt the four walls of the flat closing in on me. If only I could find time to paint, maybe I could sell some pictures and we could afford a few luxuries. We were so hard up that I'd taken to going into the fruit and vegetable store on Saturday afternoons asking if I could buy the overripe bananas for a few pence, to mash for the children. (Actually we ate them too.)

One day I saw some beautiful grapes and asked how much they were, with my mouth watering. The salesgirl gave me a withering glance. "*You* couldn't afford them." I trailed back disconsolately up the stairs to the flat with my rotten bananas.

During the holidays Sheila came to visit and completed the conquest of Shane's heart. When she left to go back to art school in Amsterdam, they were engaged.

After hearing Sheila's stories about life at the Rijksacademie art school in Amsterdam I felt deeply envious. I had been painting and drawing since I was two years old, and not being able to paint made me feel as though I had an itch that I couldn't scratch.

At last one day there was a quiet moment when Charles was asleep and Danny playing quietly. I got out my paints and started a picture. Danny saw me and came over to watch. I frowned at him. Suddenly he was not my child, he was just an obstacle in my way.

Danny put his hand on my painting. I told him "No" and took his hand off. He did it again deliberately. I gave his hand a little smack. He looked surprised and gazed at me questioningly. It was the first time I had ever hit him. He put his hand back, deliberately smearing the painting, and watching to see what I would do.

I thought, he has to learn what No means. I smacked his hand a little harder. Danny frowned and rubbed his hand in a puzzled way, but he still put his hand back defiantly. The battle continued for a few minutes until I suddenly felt sick and guilty. I knew that this was wrong. It was not the way to treat Danny.

One morning I heard Charlie crying. I rushed to the kitchen and found Danny banging Charlie's head against a stool. I snatched the baby up, but I couldn't hit Danny again. Deep inside myself I connected this with the time when I had deliberately inflicted pain on Danny by smacking his hand.

Chapter Eight

Halstead

After a year in London Jim gave up the struggle to get a second degree at the London School of Economics and applied for a new job as Work-Study Officer in Halstead, a town to the north of London.

Jim explained to me the idea behind the new towns built after the war. The town planners had wanted to avoid the kind of urban sprawl that had happened in America where New York had spread its grey concrete right down to Washington, D.C. To prevent this, the English planners decided to preserve a "green belt" of countryside around London where any further building would not be permitted. This would give city-dwellers a chance to get out into the country without having to travel too far. To allow for development they planned a ring of new towns on the other side of the green belt which could expand to take the overflow as the population increased.

Halstead was one of these new towns, and our new house was situated on the edge of the development near fields and a canal. It was a lovely house, with a fenced-in garden where the boys could play safely. We moved on Charlie's first birthday, and he took his first steps across the new lawn.

I was pleased to see that there was a French window in the living room so I would be able to paint there and keep an eye on the children at the same time.

Every room was disfigured by very ugly wallpaper crinoline ladies in the sitting-room and red and white stars in the kitchen. The hall was papered with imitation stonework. Full of exuberance, we set out to paint the walls and I over-painted them with murals, a dragon in the kitchen and a little train running along the walls of the boys' bedroom.

Jim was going to paint over the stonework paper in the hall but he was too busy, and then I had a hilarious idea, and painted a dungeon window in the stonework where two gaunt and bleeding hands clutched at some iron bars. Gran and other visitors had a good laugh at it so we let it stay until we could find the time to do more decorating, and gradually ceased to notice it anymore.

As Charles grew older he and Danny became great friends. Charlie was an easygoing child and a wonderful companion for Danny. Playing out in the garden they looked funny together: Charlie, round and comical like a little Puck with a broad grin and dimples, and white-blond hair so fine it floated when he moved, and Danny, walking with great dignity, his handsome face crowned with golden curls and his deep-blue eyes with their serious expression.

As he grew, Charlie began to change Danny's play patterns. Danny stopped jouncing up and down in his cot and began to relate to Charlie. They babbled, laughed and began to talk together. Until Charlie grew old enough to be interested in toys, Danny played with strings of safety pins with an old lavatory chain on the end. Jim referred to it jokingly as his "mayoral chain of office".

We found it funny and endearing that Danny would repeat our remarks, muttering them to himself in an undertone, like a professor committing something to memory.

Charlie talked early and this brought on Danny's speech. By the time Charlie was two, he was starting to correct his older brother. "No, Danny," he would pipe up, "You mustn't say, 'Danny wants this,' you must say, 'I want this.'"

It was the same in toilet training. Charlie watched me showing Danny how to go on the potty, then he trained himself and his brother.

One night Danny got croup. It developed so quickly; first he had a cold, then a fever, then I heard a banging noise in the boys' bedroom. I rushed upstairs and found Danny hitting his head against the wall in a panic.

"I can't breathe!" he gasped. I snatched him up and hurried downstairs; his father soothed him while I rang for an ambulance. While I rode with him to the hospital I explained to Danny that he was going to the place where they would make him better.

When we got there I begged the nurses to let me stay with him until he fell asleep. I sat by his bedside and said, "Shall I sing to you?"

Danny looked at me with dark, solemn eyes: "Sing, 'E'en though I wander far from home,'" he begged.

He was kept in hospital for three days and when his father brought him home and he saw his brother standing on the sofa, he rushed to him and hugged him round the knees, kissing his shoes, while Charlie beamed at him with his cheeky grin and laid his chubby hands on his brother's head as if in blessing.

Around this time Danny began to have nightmares. I would hear him crying in bed and go to reassure him. One night he told me that something was biting him in bed. I shook the bedclothes and showed him what it was.

"Look, it is only some apple seeds from the apple you ate in bed, remember?" From then on Danny invented a monster called "Appaseed" which gave him screaming nightmares.

Danny liked everything to stay the same. He hated furniture to be moved and he hated new clothes. If I could slip something new on him without his noticing, it would be all right once he'd worn it for a day, but if he spotted it was new, he would have a tantrum until I took it off him.

His fears took strange forms. When he and Charlie were playing in the garden, if Danny heard an aeroplane fly overhead he would run and hide in the garden shed. He wouldn't come out until the plane had gone.

Danny was nearly four years old when our third son, Thomas, was born. Danny was much more affected by this new arrival than Charles.

It was a home delivery, and the baby arrived late at night. He was three weeks overdue, so he was a beautiful chubby baby, weighing nearly ten pounds. After he was born the midwife laid him on my chest and to her astonishment he propped himself up on his elbows and looked around the room with bright, wide-open eyes.

In the morning his brothers came into the bedroom to see him. Charles was mildly interested, but Danny was deeply upset. Later that day Jim came in and asked if Danny could come into bed with me.

"Oh, can't you take the boys out for a walk?" I pleaded, feeling exhausted after the birth. But Jim came back in again and said, "The poor little fellow is just sitting outside your door all the time with his head in his hands."

I said of course Danny must come in then.

A grubby, drippy-nosed child climbed in beside me gratefully. This time Danny didn't mind me breast-feeding Thomas and he made himself useful by fetching me a drink when I needed one.

After reading books on child care I had bought a doll for the boys so that they could imitate me while I looked after the baby. They took the greatest delight in pulling it to pieces and bashing it on the floor, which must have siphoned off some of their aggression.

Soon after the birth my father arrived to visit on his way back from a business trip. He sat in an armchair and gazed at Thomas, who was a fat and contented baby. He looked round at the two other boys and said, "You've only had three children but you've managed to have more boys than I could achieve in six!"

I was so pleased to have his approval that I overlooked the implied slight to his daughters.

Now that I had three children life was hard work, but I began to make friends with other mothers who brought their babies to the local clinic. At that time, in the early '60s, women were still expected to be content to stay home, doing the housework and looking after the children. Many mothers disapproved of my wish for a painting career and asked me, "What use is painting, anyway?"

However, one of the mothers told me about a little kindergarten nearby. I was delighted at the thought of taking my two older boys there every morning and getting time to do some painting.

Danny and Charlie took to the teacher, Mrs. Meadows, a buxom, motherly lady with a kind smile. When they had been there a few months Mrs. Meadows took me aside and said that at first she'd been worried about Danny, but then she found he was very bright and he had learned to say the whole alphabet and was starting to read.

I was very pleased, sure that my "genius" theory had been proved.

Mrs. Meadows then pointed out gently that putting safety pins on children's clothes was no substitute for sewing on buttons.

I sometimes felt inadequate as a mother, but took comfort in the fact that Jim was a marvellous father to his boys. He played with them in the evenings after work and at the weekends. He got them gardening, building huts, and doing rudimentary carpentry. Charlie was his right-hand man, busy with hammer and nails, asking questions and organising Danny, who tended to be more of an interested bystander. Baby Thomas was mostly a nuisance, trying to plunge into the midst of any activity with unbridled enthusiasm.

When Jim was moved onto work-studying the town's refuse collection, there were bonuses in the shape of discarded objects which could be used as toys. One evening Jim brought home a large collection of little wooden ladders about four feet high. These made wonderful toys. The boys tried being window cleaners, holding wet rags and scrubbing; then the ladders were laid on the grass and became railways, or they were piled together to make forts.

Sometimes, when I felt adventurous, I would dress the boys up, put the baby in a pushchair, and we would go off to London for the day on the train to see art exhibitions.

My first venture was into the Wellcome Museum because the name seemed so cosy and inviting. But this was a mistake—it was full of fragile antique scientific instruments, and we were hustled out. The Royal Academy was better. There were seats there, and while the boys ate sandwiches I could scurry around and look at the pictures.

The National Gallery was better still, with lots of space and a wonderful art collection. Danny loved the paintings and became very excited when he spotted Rembrandt's painting of a man on a horse—he recognised it from an illustration in the book we were reading called "Starlight Barking."

On another expedition to a smaller gallery there was a show called "The Vienna School of Fantastic Realism." There I saw a painting that changed my life. It was called "Moses and the Burning Bush." I stood in front of it and gasped—I had never seen so much depth of feeling and skill in techniques of painting before. I stood gazing at it until the clamour of the children drove me out, but as we sat in the park and had our picnic, my mind was occupied with a plan.

I knew that this painting technique indicated the direction I needed for my own work, and dreamed that one day I would go to Vienna and study with this artist, who was called Ernst Fuchs.

Then the children called me back to the present, and I gathered up the crusts and we headed for home on the train.

As we were sitting by the window, watching the landscape fly by, Charles pointed a fat finger out of the window and asked, "What are they, Mummy?" I looked out and said, "They're street lights, dear."

"Yeth," he said, "But are they mercury vapor lights or tungsten lights?"

I was stumped. I supposed that Jim must have been giving him a lecture on street lighting.

Meanwhile the old gentleman opposite us in the carriage had burst out laughing.

Just as Danny never played with toys but preferred strings of safety pins instead, so Charles also could not be bothered much with toys. He carried around a box of plugs and light bulbs, which he used under his father's supervision. He said proudly that he was going to be a 'lectrician when he grew up.

One day he disobeyed his father's instructions and was playing with a lamp unsupervised. He got a nasty electric shock, which taught him a lesson and frightened me horribly. After that he carried around a box of different spare parts, and when I asked about them he said soberly, "I'm going to be a plumber."

When I had a moment free, I wrote to my mother and told her about the wonderful painting I had seen by Ernst Fuchs, and said that one day I wanted to study with him in Vienna. I tended to write Mother a lot asking for advice on bringing up the children.

She had been an enthusiastic convert to Catholicism, so, remembering my childhood, I thought I'd better start teaching the boys some religion. I didn't want to talk about Hell and damnation that the nuns had frightened us with, so I tried to speak only of God's love. I told them they didn't need to fear death, and carried away by my imagination, I said that death would only be like God coming in a golden chariot to take them to Heaven.

I bought them little Mass books to take to church, but when Danny saw the picture of the Crucifixion inside the cover he turned a greenish color and looked as though he was going to faint.

"The pins!" he cried. "They put the pins in his hands!"

I tried to comfort him but he turned his face to the wall and wouldn't speak to me.

Chapter Nine

Troubles

At four and a half, Danny was due to start school in September. I dreaded the day. Danny still seemed too raw and vulnerable. I took him there, all dressed up in school tie, blazer and trousers. The mothers all clustered by the gate; we weren't allowed to stay with the children and settle them in.

The teacher had a very hard face, and several mothers said she'd been moved from another school because she was so strict; one mother whispered that she specially hated boys because she'd been jilted by a man. Yet she had been put with the youngest children! I felt sick with apprehension.

Danny didn't seem to like school. He was so reluctant to go that I allowed him to stay home for a day. My mother had always been very free and easy about school attendance; she looked on schools as a necessary evil.

"Does he have to go?" I asked Jim that night. I couldn't see why a small child should be made so miserable.

But Jim was annoyed that I'd kept Danny home. He had never really approved of my bohemian family and now he became quite firm. He pointed out that it was the law of the land that children had to go to school. Danny was not to be mollycoddled and made into a sissy; it was time he went out into the world and learned to conform.

Next morning with a heavy heart I dressed Danny in his school clothes and took him to school. Danny begged me not to make him go. He knelt down in the street and put his arms around my knees and cried.

I was full of fears, afraid of disobeying my husband, afraid of the laws in this strange country, and above all afraid of things I didn't understand in Danny. In desperation I forced Danny to go, feeling a strange hardening of my heart.

When I got home again I telephoned another primary school nearby to see if they would take Danny instead perhaps he might like it better there but the headmistress said that they were full, and I could hear her amusement at the sound of tears in my voice.

From the morning when I rejected his cry for help, Danny became cold towards me. One day I heard screaming and rushed to the kitchen to find Danny methodically slapping Thomas's face as he sat in his high chair. My hand flew out and I smacked Danny across the face in a rage. I snatched up the baby to comfort him.

Then I went to find Danny. I tried to talk to him. I said that he must never do that again. He must love his little brother.

"I don't love him," said Danny. I told him I only wanted him to be good because I loved him.

"I don't love you," Danny said. "I don't love anybody." His small face was white and rigid.

Soon after that we had a phone call from the school. A woman said that Danny was behaving strangely and we must take him to the psychiatrist at the Watford Clinic. She insisted that when we got the appointment both my husband and I must be there. In the meantime Danny could stay at home.

A week later we took Danny to the Watford Clinic. Danny was led away and we waited for a long time, feeling more and more anxious until we were called into the psychiatrist's office to hear his report.

He sat smiling behind his desk looking at us through his steel-rimmed glasses.

"You have a remarkable son there!" he said. We both felt relieved. So it wasn't going to be bad news after all.

We waited and he regarded us both with an unwavering smile. Then he spoke: "He's schizophrenic," he said.

His words hit us like bullets; we were totally unprepared. I couldn't think or move. There was nothing in my head big enough to wrap around those words and incorporate them into my life. Part of the horror was the strange feeling that this man had got some kind of kick out of giving us this shock.

Through a fog I heard him telling us that he had made an appointment for Danny at the Maudsley Hospital in London to have his diagnosis confirmed, but that he was sure he was right.

Somehow we got ourselves and Danny home. We could not speak much to each other. After a while I began to feel sick and went to bed, covering up my head under the blankets. Surely, I thought, if God sees that I can't bear this, then He will take it away.

Jim looked after the children for the weekend, but on Monday he had to go to work. I saw that he looked exhausted. I felt deeply ashamed. The blow had fallen on him too, and I had left him with three boys to look after. I got up and took on the household chores again, but I was in the grip of a deep despair, which I pushed aside under the carpet of my conscious mind while I became obsessed by Danny's problem and gave only perfunctory attention to the needs of my two smaller sons.

After further tests at the Child Guidance Clinic in Halstead we were notified by the educational authorities that Danny was to go to the local E.S.N. School for educationally subnormal children. They explained that this school had smaller classes and could give Danny the attention that he needed. I put him on the special bus every morning and collected him at lunchtime. It was felt that half a day would be enough for him at first.

Danny hated this school. He said the other children were "funny." He had a great aversion to illness or deformity.

One day when we were walking home from the bus with the other two boys, Danny suddenly stopped and his face went red. He gave a groan and then burst into laughter. I stared at him, puzzled.

"Are you having a joke, Danny? What is it?" I asked.

Danny didn't answer. He seemed confused, and then embarrassed when I questioned him.

During the next few days he repeated this performance. I rang the Child Guidance Clinic to ask them what this meant. I thought it might be some horrible manifestation of his schizophrenia, but the woman psychologist there had an explanation. "There is a girl at the E.S.N. school who suffers from epilepsy. No doubt Danny has been fascinated by her and is imitating her."

Danny's "imitations" became more and more theatrical. At mealtimes he would seize the table and groan, gripping the edge of the table until his knuckles were white. Then he would then laugh and breathe so heavily that he seemed on the verge of losing consciousness.

I couldn't understand why he wanted to imitate this epileptic child so often. Was his fear of deformity and illness leading to a deadly fascination? There was nothing I could do to distract him from these imitations, and they were occurring with greater and greater frequency.

One day I noticed that they were happening at exactly two-hour intervals. I went cold with fear; this was uncanny.

How could any child, however disturbed, time himself so exactly? Was this a strange form of madness?

I rang the headmaster of the E.S.N. school to ask for more details about the child Danny had been imitating. The headmaster was mystified. "But your son comes in the morning, and she comes in the afternoon. He has never seen her!"

He suggested that I ring my local doctor, Dr. Sutton. I made an appointment for that evening. The doctor's surgery was crowded with people and Danny ran wild, but I couldn't find the energy to control him. I just sat staring at the carpet, waiting for the next blow to fall. The pattern on the carpet seemed to burn itself into my brain in the eternity that we waited.

At last it was our turn. Dr. Sutton gave me one sharp glance and told me to sit down. He made me blow my nose. Then he said I was to tell him the whole story from the beginning.

"But there's a queue of people out there!" I said. I couldn't really believe he wanted to listen.

"To hell with the queue of people!" he said, looking at Danny who was fingering the clock calendar on his desk and asking questions about it. When I'd finished telling him what had happened he said angrily: "They've no right to go saying things like that about him! Schizophrenic indeed! At four years old! It's the psychiatrists that want their heads examined!"

He snorted in disgust and reached for a pad of paper. "I'll write them a letter!" He smiled grimly, "I'll cut their legs off from them!"

This wiry, intelligent man appeared to me like a knight in shining armour. The heavens seemed to open again, and there was hope! Nevertheless there were things I didn't understand.

"But ... but Danny is doing such strange things!" I said, and described Danny's "imitations."

Dr. Sutton examined Danny for a long time. "He's epileptic," he told me, "he's having fits. That's all that's wrong with him."

Chapter Ten

The Maudsley Hospital

It was difficult to stop Danny's fits. Dr. Sutton put him on phenobarbitone at first; Danny's fits grew less frequent but he staggered around half asleep all the time. Then as his system adjusted to the medication, the fits began to get worse. He often fell to the ground in convulsions.

Now that Danny's fits were obvious and unpleasant to see, people began to avoid us, as if they feared that our misfortune might be catching. Friends and neighbours who had been kind in the past began acting strangely. One neighbour said that Danny shouldn't be allowed out, another friend insisted that Danny was putting it on to get attention.

Dr. Sutton became my chief support. I kept trotting Danny back and forth to his surgery to pour out my troubles, hoping desperately that something could be found to help him.

One day I was rewarded. Dr. Sutton told me that a new drug for epilepsy had been discovered called Epanutin. It changed Danny's life, controlling the fits without making him sleepy. Danny's fits ceased altogether and he looked like a normal boy again.

Meanwhile, the psychiatrist at the Watford Clinic had made an appointment for Danny at the Maudsley Hospital in London so that his diagnosis of schizophrenia could be confirmed.

On the appointed day we took Danny there where he was examined intensively over many days. Jim and I were also examined, and questioned for hours. We had to go over every detail of Danny's life. We didn't know what they were looking for, and they were often impatient with us. It was hard to pick out what they wanted from the details that came flooding back.

Yes, we assured them, Danny had been a wanted baby.

Yes, there were complications during pregnancy.

Yes, he had odd habits.

One younger, rather handsome man asked how Danny handled himself physically. "Well, he's not very dexterous," I admitted. He gave me a scornful look. "You mean he's clumsy."

The psychiatrists wrote everything down and had a discussion among themselves. Then they spoke to us.

We discovered that there might have been brain damage at birth, that Danny's love of playing with pins instead of toys was a kind of fetishism, that his repeating overheard sentences to himself was called echolalia and was one of the signs of autism. Our fond personal memories of Danny's childhood were stripped away and all we were left with were medical labels.

They questioned us further about our family histories: Was there any epilepsy in either family? No, we assured them, no record of epilepsy as far back as we could trace. What about mental illness? I had to admit that my mother's father, who had died before I was born, had been mentally ill.

They nodded to themselves and made more notes. Then they discussed Danny's maladjustment at school.

"We think now," said a younger psychiatrist, "that some children actually don't understand words spoken to them in a strange place like school. To them it is as if everyone is talking in a strange language."

"Oh, yes!" I said suddenly, "It is like that." I remembered my first time in kindergarten where I had been left in a huge dim hall, with Sister Tarsissius speaking to me in a sharp voice, but I couldn't grasp the words. Remembering my misery then, I felt a terrible pang that I had forced Danny to go to school against his will.

The visits to the Maudsley Hospital continued over several days. My husband could not take off the time from work, so I took Danny into London while my next-door neighbour minded the two youngest boys. I sat for hours in the waiting room. The psychiatrists couldn't seem to agree amongst themselves about Danny. Different doctors led Danny away each day to do tests on him.

I watched him getting stiff and withdrawn in front of all these psychiatrists; it was as if he were reading their minds and beginning to become what they expected him to be. Instead of the lively, active boy he was at home, he would emerge zombie-like from the various psychological sandpits and tests.

The stress of all these tests on Danny showed itself in the renewal of his fits. It happened in the long lunch break between sessions. We'd had lunch at a cafe and had stepped inside a china shop where we were looking at the ornaments. Suddenly Danny stiffened, went rigid, and fell backwards like a lead soldier.

As he hit the ground with a crash, every ornament in the shop tinkled and clattered. By a miracle Danny wasn't hurt, nor were any of the goods damaged, but the lady in the shop couldn't get us out fast enough.

In the afternoon I waited again until the young psychiatrist led Danny back to me. He explained to me that because of his condition, my son would never be able to read.

This was too much. "But he *can* read!" I said angrily. The young man gave me a pitying smile. Like Danny, I could read what he was thinking: Here is a typical hysterical mother, unable to face the facts. I was furious.

"Look, I'll prove it," I said. "I'll show you that Danny can read." I sat him on my lap and picked up one of the battered children's books that were lying on the table for the children in the waiting room.

Danny was reluctant to respond at first, feeling my tension, but at last he relaxed enough to become interested in the game, and as I pointed to a word, he would read it aloud.

I looked up triumphantly at the psychiatrist, who shrugged.

"You've made him memorise the book," he said. "He's not reading the words at all."

I longed to fling the grubby book into his handsome arrogant face.

"This is one of your own books!" I cried. "Danny has never seen it before!"

Then I saw with despair that his face was shut. He wasn't going to believe me. And Danny's whole future might depend on this man's verdict. It was frightening that he didn't seem to want to find out the real truth, but only wanted Danny to fit neatly into his theories.

I wondered if perhaps they had been angered by Dr. Sutton's scathing letter, and were all the more determined to prove that Danny was schizophrenic.

Even the older psychiatrists seemed to be no better. I felt deeply dissatisfied as the tests drew to a close; I felt that none of them had really seen Danny as he was. I knew he had a potential that they weren't seeing.

One day I begged a few of them to come and see Danny at home. "If you saw him there where he is relaxed you could see him as he really is!" There was a silence as they all stared at me in amazement. It was as if one of the performing monkeys had asked the head zookeepers to tea!

At last we were informed that all the tests were over, and my husband and I were to come to the Maudsley Hospital for the final verdict. As we trudged towards the hospital with Danny, Jim remarked, "At least we'll know what is wrong with him now."

All the psychiatrists were gathered together for the meeting. They were still arguing. Many said that Danny was completely unresponsive, but one older man took out a ball and threw it at Danny and he caught it.

"This proves that he is responsive," he argued. He turned to us both and said, "Although your son exhibits many of the symptoms of autism and schizophrenia, there are important areas where he differs. We have had many discussions and we have come to the conclusion that for the present, we just don't know." He went on to say that they would report back to the education authorities who would decide what education Danny would receive.

Meanwhile Danny stayed at home. He was five years old now and he became obsessed by numbers. He counted all day and did endless sums on paper, doubling the numbers each time so the numbers reached into the thousands and then millions. He wrote on any paper he could find: old paper bags, newspapers and walls; everything was covered with the ever-increasing sums.

I knew it was compulsive behaviour, yet I felt that the fact that he was getting these huge sums right showed that he was more intelligent than the psychiatrists realised.

At last we received word that a psychiatric social worker was coming to the house. I was overjoyed. At last someone in authority would see Danny in his own environment. I cleaned up the house, dressed up the children, and laid out teacups.

There was a knock on the door and I opened it to a nicely dressed middle-aged lady. I greeted her cordially, but to my surprise she turned white, and backed away nervously.

My eyes followed her gaze, and to my horror I saw the dungeon window I had painted over the stone wallpaper many years before, with the gaunt skeletal hands gripping the bars and blood dripping down. We had forgotten to paint over it.

Chapter Eleven

Mrs. Watt

It took quite a while for the psychiatric social worker, whose name was Mrs. Dearden, to have any confidence in me after that, but she called in one day unexpectedly at Christmastime and saw the Christmas tree lit up and the presents scattered around and the boys at play (and the unfortunate mural painted over), and finally she relaxed and we became friends.

She saw a portrait I was doing of Danny and remarked, "You know, you are lucky to have the means of expressing yourself, I'm sure it must help. I've seen so many mothers who have the same problems as you, but they have no way of expressing themselves."

At first I felt a bit ruffled as if she were treating my painting as mere occupational therapy. But then I reflected that it was not belittling art to say that it helped one work through one's problems, and maybe I could paint out my feelings so that I would be better able to accept and understand Danny's situation.

Danny seemed to be in my thoughts all the time. A part of me felt that I could *will* him to be normal and healthy. Jim, on the other hand, seemed fairly despondent about his eldest son.

I asked Mrs. Dearden about this and she said, "The mother's role is not affected by sickness in a child. It is a nursing and caring role, and therefore the more sick a child is, the more a mother can express her love. But the father's role is to be an agent of growth. If something affects the growth of that child, then the father's role is affected and his relationship with the child becomes more difficult."

Another problem was troubling me. After we found out that Danny had so many problems, we didn't want to risk having another child. We had been lucky with Charles and Thomas but there could be problems again if we had a fourth child.

I had always been an obedient Catholic, anxious to keep to the rules and get that reserved place in Heaven we'd been promised, but Jim no longer agreed with the ideas of the Catholic Church and soon he stopped going to church altogether. We had tried the system known as "Vatican roulette" where the body temperature is taken and the "infertile" times made use of, and Thomas was the result.

With the support of our sympathetic parish priest, Father Foster, I decided to go on the pill. This solved our problems but gave me occasional pangs of guilt whenever I heard a hard-line Catholic talking. One day when I was particularly worried about Danny, I went to Church and lit some candles and prayed.

A sympathetic looking woman came up to me and asked if she could help. Stupidly, I poured out my problems, and she said: "Have you ever thought that your son's illness could be God's punishment because you are on the pill?"

Luckily Father Foster was more open-minded and he started a parish discussion group where parishioners could get together and discuss the spiritual implications of the pill. After several meetings it was decided unanimously that as the celibate clergy didn't have to sleep in a double bed with a woman every night, they were in no position to understand the situation.

Meanwhile Danny was not getting any better. One night when he was having a bad fit in bed, we were settling him down when we saw Charles in the next bed watching with round frightened eyes.

Afterwards Jim said, "It isn't right for Charles to share a room with Danny now he's having so many fits. Let's move Thomas into Danny's bed and give Danny the little room to himself."

The new arrangement worked well. Danny was pleased to have a room all to himself, and sharing a room brought the two younger boys closer together.

Charles, now five years old, became more lighthearted; he had been too responsible for Danny, and Thomas at three years old became more of a companion to him. They were completely different in character, and argued from morning till night. Thomas seemed to have been born talking. He would try to join conversations by babbling loudly even before he knew any words. Whenever I went shopping with him in his pushchair he would call out to the passersby, "Hello, man! Hello, lady! Say hello man! Say hello lady!"

He always met with an enthusiastic response, which was sometimes inconvenient for me when I wasn't feeling sociable and only wanted to scurry out and grab a loaf of bread.

I started a painting of the children round the table eating red jelly for tea. It was a time when they were comparatively quiet. I figured that if I worked on it a little every day, I would have a painting at the end. So every afternoon I set out the bowls of red jelly, until after a week Tommy took one look at the red jelly in the bowl and started to cry, and the older boys began throwing it at each other.

Danny, at six years old, didn't go to school. We were still waiting to hear from the educational authorities. So every morning he watched Charles go to school with the other boys while he stayed at home with Tommy. Then one day we got a letter to say that an educational psychologist was coming to test him.

I dreaded another forceful mind-dissecter barging in to impose his views on poor Danny, but when this psychologist arrived everything was different. First of all, she was a woman, Miss Sandy, and though she was tall she was so gentle and quiet that she didn't seem to take up any space. She sat in the living room and watched the boys playing, and soon they forgot she was there. Then very softly she spoke to Danny, and it was almost like magic! It was as if she retreated deep into herself and called to Danny from there. I hadn't known anyone could do that. For the first time in his life, Danny responded to a stranger. Instead of going silent and cold as he had done at the clinics, he answered, shyly at first, then with more confidence. Soon she had him laughing and doing her tests as if they were a game. The only problem was fending off the other boys, who wanted to play too.

After a while Miss Sandy said, "Danny was not what I was expecting. I believe he is highly intelligent. I would like you to bring him to my office to do more tests." Later at her office she confirmed her first impression. She showed us how Danny was doing the tests with ease.

"He is brilliant!" she said. "At six years old he has the intelligence of a boy of twelve! He should never have been sent to the E.S.N. school; it was quite the wrong place for him."

Jim looked as though a great weight had been lifted from his shoulders, and he beamed at his eldest son. We both felt jubilant. This proved that Dr. Sutton was right Danny would be fine now that his potential had been recognised. I even thought to myself that my theory that Danny was a genius might have been right after all!

Meanwhile Miss Sandy had been reflecting. At last she said, "I think that for the moment your son would benefit from a home tutor. I think I know just the right person."

That was how Mrs. Watt came into Danny's life; a beautiful woman and a gifted teacher. Danny was very susceptible to female charms and his shyness with her wore off rapidly. Soon they settled into a good working relationship and Danny made rapid progress.

Jim was very interested in Danny's scholastic progress. He transformed Danny's bedroom into a schoolroom by putting up shelves and a desk.

Danny grew very attached to Mrs. Watt. She was always patient, kind and deeply honest. Danny, with his vulnerable openness to people, could always detect lying. Together they studied, made scrapbooks and went on nature rambles. Danny's face became happy and animated, and he stopped having fits.

Chapter Twelve

Pills

When Danny had not had a single fit for months, we began to wonder if perhaps he was growing out of them. We both hated giving him nine pills every day. Jim said one morning, "Do you still think he needs to take all those pills?"

Gran on her visits deplored the fact that Danny had to take so much medication. Dr. Sutton had prescribed them, but after all, doctors tend to believe in pills.

My mother and father were now living in Switzerland. Mother was a great believer in natural healing and the curative power of raw food. She wrote asking if it were really necessary for Danny to take so many pills when he was only six years old. She asked us why we didn't try alternative medicine.

She offered to pay for Danny and me to go to a clinic in Zurich which specialised in curing through the healing powers in raw food. We would stay two weeks there and meanwhile she would come to England to look after the other two boys.

I begged Jim to let us go, but he was unenthusiastic. At last he shrugged his shoulders and said, "I suppose you might as well go if you want to. It won't do any good, but at least it won't do any harm."

I wrote back joyfully to say we could go. The trip would take place in four months when it would be early February. Meanwhile I could hardly bear to go on feeding Danny his pills when he seemed so well. I began to try leaving out one every day.

After two weeks, Danny had a grand mal seizure, falling to the ground in convulsions. I took him straight to Dr. Sutton's surgery and confessed what I had done. He gave me a blistering lecture which I never forgot, and from that day I never attempted to interfere with Danny's dosage. But the damage had been done, I had disturbed the balance of the medication and during the weeks that followed, Danny's fits went on increasing, out of control. When he saw how distressed I was, Dr. Sutton told me that in all probability Danny's fits would have started up again once he began to outgrow the dosage. Nevertheless, I could not forgive myself.

Danny was put on a much higher dosage, and still the fits kept on increasing. At last Dr. Sutton felt he should be examined by a specialist. He arranged an appointment for Danny at the Maida Vale Hospital for Nervous Diseases.

I took Danny down there and we had to sit in a bleak waiting room with nothing for a child to do. Danny hated hospitals by now and became more and more restless and angry. After three hours of waiting I could no longer control him, and he ran wildly around the hospital with the nurses chasing after him. One of the nurses scolded me and I told her we'd been waiting over three hours. She went away to speak to someone and we were seen without any more delay. Danny's bad behaviour had its uses.

By now I was exhausted and the specialist began to bark questions at me with great speed. I hesitated and became confused. This seemed to put him in a rage and he began to yell at me. I broke down in floods of tears. He stopped and looked at me irritably, trying to speak more gently to this half-witted hysterical mother.

After he examined Danny he became kinder.

"Your son is having fits all the time!" he told me. "They are not apparent as they are only petit mal, but they are affecting him continually."

After that consultation, Danny had to take still more drugs, including a new one called Mysoline. The Mysoline seemed to stop his fits for a while, but it changed his character. At night he would tear magazines and newspapers into tiny fragments so that every morning his bed was covered in confetti. But the daytime was much worse. He became like a mischievous imp. The moment my back was turned he would smash something, or scatter ashes on the carpet, or take a stick and go out to hit other children.

I grew to dread the sound of a knock at the door; it was usually a neighbour come to complain that Danny had attacked her child.

One evening after the children had gone to bed, Mr. Martin, a man from the lane near us, called and asked if he could talk to us. He explained that his children had been complaining to him about Danny hitting them but he wanted to tell us that he understood. He was epileptic himself. He had always appeared to be a shy, reticent man, but now he opened his heart to us. He told us his life story. He had been on Phenobarbitone all his life. It had affected his appearance. Because of his fits the only job he could get was that of assistant gardener. We tried to listen sympathetically, but all the time we longed for him to go. We hadn't yet come to terms with what was happening to Danny. There were things we didn't want to think about and this man was a living reminder of them. We were determined that Danny would have a better life than his had been.

Shortly after this, as Jim and I were walking along the canal, we rounded a corner we saw Mr. Martin ahead, walking slowly. We looked at each other. It would have been right to go and talk to him, but we backed away not wanting to be with him. He seemed a spectre of what Danny might become. As we retreated I realised that he had seen us—his face was visible for a moment, deeply hurt, and then he turned and I saw his bent back shuffling off into the distance. Often the sight came back to haunt me in my dreams.

Mrs. Watt found teaching Danny very difficult now that he was so troublesome. She suggested that having a pet might help him. We got a cat, but Danny wasn't interested. One morning he threw it out of the upper window. Luckily the poor animal was unharmed.

What was strange was that as he became more disruptive, Danny began to take an interest in music. We bought a second-hand piano and arranged music lessons for him. He would sit for hours playing the piano, which was wonderful because then I knew that he wasn't getting into trouble.

At this time a kindly parishioner came to visit. She earnestly begged me to consider sending Danny to Lourdes. "If you storm heaven with your prayers," she said, "God will have to listen."

I felt terribly weary as I listened to her speech. I had been down that road before.

I had stormed heaven with my prayers so that Jim would become a Catholic, and they had been answered, but over the years I came to see that it hadn't been right for Jim to convert to my religion. It went against his nature and upbringing, and gradually he had ceased to go to any church at all. I felt it would have been better if I had been able to accept the differences in our faiths from the beginning. I didn't want to demand things from God anymore; instead I felt it would be better to try to find out what His purpose was instead of trying to overrule Him all the time. Surely He must have had a purpose for Danny's life!

One day as we were eating a lunch of spaghetti, Danny had a bad fit at table, smearing the spaghetti all over himself and on the floor. I carried him to the sofa and settled him down—he usually dozed off after a fit. Instead, this time he got up like a zombie, went to the table, sat down to eat and promptly had another fit, just as messy as the first.

The two younger boys began to cry. It was too much. I scolded Charlie, telling him he should be looking after his younger brother, then I carried Danny once again to the sofa, where he seemed to be having yet one more fit. Terrified, I phoned Dr. Sutton. He came and examined Danny, and said that he was afraid that perhaps Danny had a brain tumour. He assured us that if there was one it could be removed, but it was imperative to find it quickly.

He arranged for Danny to go to the Great Ormond Street Hospital for Children. Danny stayed there a week and was examined thoroughly, but no tumour was found. When we visited him in hospital we saw the saddest cases: a pretty ten-year-old girl called Sally, who was having grand mal seizures every ten minutes, and a brave young boy who was about to undergo his third brain operation. These children seemed to put our problems in perspective.

Jim drove Danny home at last and he arrived in clouds of glory; he had been car-sick on the way home when there was no time to stop, and then had a fit and smeared the mess over everything.

This inauspicious return home was followed by more bad behaviour, but this time something began to click inside my mind. It was out of character for Danny to behave so maliciously. Could it be the Mysoline tablets?

I went to Dr. Sutton to see if my hunch was right. He agreed that it might be, and put Danny on different tablets, including a new one called Tegretol.

That very evening Danny began to change. He saw the cat on the kitchen table licking the butter and began to laugh. As I watched him I realised that he hadn't laughed for the two months that he had been on the Mysoline tablets. All that evening and all night he kept breaking into laughter and crowing, "The cat licked the butter!"

Jim and I looked at each other in horror; had Danny just exchanged one weird pattern of behaviour for another? However, by morning Danny had settled down to being a normal happy boy. The only sad thing was that he never again touched the piano.

Mrs. Watt was delighted at the change in Danny; "I don't know how much longer I could have gone on teaching him as he was!" she admitted.

But my worries weren't over. Ever since Danny had come back from hospital he had been writing peculiar notes. At first I assumed it was part of the trouble with the Mysoline tablets, but it didn't cease when they were changed. The notes read like a textbook Oedipus complex; they said "I love Mummy" or "I am going to marry Mummy" or "I am going to kill Daddy."

Sick with anxiety I brought Danny and his notes to Dr. Sutton. It now appeared that Danny might be insane after all.

I showed the notes to the Doctor and told him of this new development. He asked me, "Didn't they tell you at the hospital that his brain would be disturbed by the brain scan they were using to test him?"

I shook my head dumbly. Dr. Sutton's brow was like thunder. "Well, they damn well should have!" he declared. "Putting you through all this worry for nothing! He'll be right as rain in a week or so."

Chapter Thirteen

Zurich

At last it was time for me to take Danny to the health clinic in Switzerland. I had been looking forward more and more to getting away. With all the anxiety of the last few months, I had begun to feel trapped in a cage of misery; just the thought of getting away and traveling to a new country was a relief, and on top of that I fantasised about a magical diet which would mean a complete recovery for Danny.

My mother arrived, beaming with goodwill and enthusiasm. She had brought the air tickets for Danny and me, and had paid in advance for our stay at the clinic. But suddenly Jim turned against the whole plan. He argued with me until late in the night. He said Danny had been through too much lately. He didn't want him to be taken there to be poked and prodded at by more doctors. He asked me not to go.

I felt torn in two. My mother was so happy to be doing this for us, she had planned it all so carefully. I could also see that Jim had a point; Danny *had* been through a lot in the last few weeks.

At last we reached a compromise: We would go to Zurich, but it would just be a holiday for Danny; no doctors would do anything to him. I felt guilty at going against my husband's wishes, and it made a small rift between us.

Mrs. Watt had prepared Danny for the trip by doing geography lessons on Switzerland, and she asked us to save all the travel documents and little things like tram tickets so she and Danny could make a record of our journey together. Danny seemed to have outgrown his dislike of change and looked forward to the trip.

He enjoyed the excitement of traveling and was interested in all the details of the plane journey. We arrived at the clinic without any difficulty. It was an attractive building, set in a pretty landscape of Swiss mountains. The clinic was well run and had a pleasant atmosphere. Danny and I shared a room and had each other's exclusive company for two weeks.

Being alone with Danny for so long, I began to see things I had never guessed before. I saw that I had been obsessed with Danny's problems, which had the effect of making me want to find distractions all the time.

Now that I was forced to be alone with him, I had to form a relationship with the real Danny, who was neither the ideal child that I longed him to be nor the dreaded insane child that I feared so much.

He was himself, with a character of his own. He had inherited his father's interest in history and politics, and his love of artistic things from me. He had a shrewd way of assessing people and an unexpected quiet sense of humor that was very Irish.

I also noticed he liked to have his own way. He loved the fact that he had me to himself and basked in my full attention, so much so that he objected whenever I turned my attention away from him. In the evening he would retire to bed only if I went too, in the twin bed next to his. If I tried to read, he objected, saying the light kept him awake. I took to reading under the blankets with a torch. However in the daytime he was a delightful companion. We went for walks, looking at the old buildings in the town. We rode on the funicular railway, and tried ice skating together.

At the clinic the hospital atmosphere was maintained by a visit from a nurse in a white coat. She knocked on our bedroom door every night and asked in a sinister voice, "Heff you hed stool today?"

Danny took part in some gymnastics which were run by a pretty young girl. He was not examined as Jim had stipulated, but occasionally he would be served with some herbal remedies in addition to our whole food and raw food meals. One morning he was served a glassful of what looked like frog-spawn. Danny took one look and refused to have anything to do with it.

I apologised to the Swiss waitress who came to clear our table: "I'm afraid my son won't eat this."

She stared at the contents and exclaimed, "I don't blame him!"

Despite the healthy food, there was no miraculous cure for Danny at the clinic, but by the time we were due to leave, Danny and I had formed a new relationship—we had become friends.

I came back refreshed by the trip and thanked my mother gratefully, but the most touching tribute she had came from Danny, who wrote notes to her and left them all over the house where she could find them; they just said, "Thank you, Granny."

Mother was delighted at Danny's response. She'd had a difficult time with my other two sons, as they were so different from American children. She was devoted to the cult of raw food and wanted to put them on a health diet of mainly uncooked fruit and vegetables, but they were not enthusiastic.

"But then," she said, "when I suggested some kind of treat and asked them, Would you like ice cream for dessert?, they just said, I don't mind. So I told them if they didn't mind, I won't bother!" snorted Mother indignantly. I explained that the boys were English and this was an example of the English understatement, but Mother wasn't convinced.

However, she must have made an impression on Tommy, because when he got his next instalment of pocket money he came back from the shops with a health loaf instead of sweets as usual. Jim was very amused. "Heredity will out," he said.

Before Mother left she asked me when the older boys were going to make their First Communion, and I realised that as they weren't going to a Catholic school, I would have to prepare them myself. So I started a religious class for Danny and Charlie, who were to make their First Communion together in May at a Mass in our house said by Father Foster, our parish priest.

But when I spoke to the boys about Confession and examination of conscience, Danny looked miserable and went up to his room. I followed him and asked him why he looked unhappy.

"Because I'm so bad," he said.

"Why do you think you are bad, Danny?" I asked in surprise.

"I went out and hit all the children, and I broke things!" he said.

Then I realised that Danny was remembering the time when he was on Mysoline tablets all those months ago. He was blaming himself for what he had done then under the influence of those pills. I felt very neglectful that I hadn't thought before this to explain and reassure him. He had carried that burden of guilt all this time!

I sat down beside him and hugged him. "Listen, Danny, you were on some pills that were bad for you, the Mysoline tablets, do you remember? They affected your brain and made you want to do those things, so it wasn't your fault, and nobody blames you at all."

He looked up at me, his face cleared, and he gave me a relieved smile.

Chapter Fourteen

Palpitations

At last Danny settled down into a normal routine. The Tegretol tablets seemed to stabilise him, and although he had a few very light fits from time to time, in all other respects he was happy and busy.

While I was teaching my children about religion, I was reassessing things in my own mind. My older sister had dedicated her life to God and was in Africa, founding schools and colleges. She was very upset when she heard that I was on the pill, and wrote to try to persuade me to obey the laws of the Catholic Church. "Can't you at least have one more child?" she begged.

I wrote back to say that even if I had one more child I would still go back to using the pill, so I might as well be hanged for a lamb as a sheep! But I also tried to tell her what I was beginning to feel, that an obsession with rules was the wrong way to God.

"Do you remember when we were children we used to pretend that the big blue carpet in Granny's room was the sea, and the red Oriental rugs on it were rafts? We were very upset if one of us weren't on a red rug, and made poor Granny get up and move her chair on to one so that she'd be safe. Isn't your wish to have me keep the rules on the same kind of level?"

Something that reinforced my dislike of the rule-keepers was hearing Mrs. Johnson, a woman from our parish, talk about her neighbour, who was a Catholic who admitted she was using birth control. Mrs. Johnson, the mother of five boisterous children, was scathing about her.

"When I saw her coming back from Communion I said to myself, "Well, my only comfort is that she'll go straight to Hell when she dies!""

It came to me that I could not worship the God that this woman believed in.

A neighbouring family asked me to baby-sit for them. I was afraid to refuse as it seemed churlish, yet I really did not have enough time in the day for my own life, let alone for doing favours for other people. In the end I grew to hate them so much I went to Father Foster and said tearfully, "I hate my neighbour!" He asked why and I told him about the baby-sitting. "I don't like to refuse them and now I can't stand them!"

"Can't you tell them you don't like doing this?" he asked. I was taken aback. I had never thought of such a simple solution. "You see," he said, "you placate people too much."

"You mean it's bad for me?" I asked.

He nodded. "It's bad for them as well. We placate because we don't want to have a bad image of ourselves." He smiled and added, "I remember when I saw that I was doing this, I decided to try the opposite. It's difficult with people you know, but you could try being rude to people on buses to begin with."

I was tickled by this novel idea. I wasn't courageous enough to carry it out, but next time the neighbours asked me to baby-sit I was able to tell them I couldn't do it; they accepted this, and my hatred ceased.

Another thing which I found hard to face was my revulsion when Danny had a fit. When his face became distorted and purple as he convulsed I was repelled by its ugliness. I knew this was wicked and unmotherly.

I asked Father Foster, "How can I be so unfeeling?"

He said it was a natural reaction, especially for an artist who is primarily a visual person. "Perhaps it is a good thing for you to see and experience," he said. "The qualities of compassion and mercy are being forged in you."

I thought rebelliously that if it took Danny's suffering to forge those qualities in me, then it was too high a price to pay. I wasn't worth that. I would rather have had Danny well.

One night I woke up with my heart hammering in my chest. I began to panic as the heartbeats went faster and faster until I thought I would faint. I went out of the room quietly so as not to disturb my sleeping husband, and battled this dreadful condition until morning. Then I asked Jim to drive me to the doctor. By now I was sure I was having a heart attack and maybe going to die.

Dr. Sutton listened to my heart with his stethoscope. It was pounding so hard it was difficult for me to breathe.

"Is it a heart attack?" I gasped. He gave me a reassuring smile. "No, you have got palpitations."

"What are they?" I asked, still convinced I was going to die.

"It is just a reaction to the strain you have been under with your son. I will give you tranquillisers to tide you over for a while." I couldn't understand this. "But Danny's all right now!" I said. "He's happy with Mrs. Watt. Why am I having this now?"

Dr. Sutton looked up from the prescription he was writing out. "It often happens like that. Once your strength is no longer needed you can afford to break down."

He hesitated, then laid down his pen and continued, "To tell the truth, when you came into my surgery that first evening I was more worried about you than Danny. Now don't worry, you'll be all right. You just need to take these for a while."

I took the prescription reluctantly. I'd heard of women getting addicted to tranquillisers. On the other hand I couldn't face another night like the last one.

The tranquillisers prevented a renewal of the palpitations, but in a peculiar way they seemed to distance me from life.

Sometimes I would sit at the kitchen table and churn everything over in my mind. Dr. Sutton's kindly remark that he had been worried about me began to take on a terrifying dimension. I began to wiggle my mind the way I used to wiggle a sore tooth, to make it hurt. What if I were insane? Perhaps it was hereditary and Danny had got it from me? What if it were all inside me waiting to come out? Then I felt an inner explosion and thought I would faint; my heart started to pound again and I would take more tranquillisers.

From then on I lived in fear of myself. I was tortured by the thought of madness. I never forgot my husband's support and kindness at this time, but it did not make me well. I needed desperately to find a point of stability in myself.

So many of my props had been kicked away. I was in a strange country away from my parents. I had seen myself as a Cinderella who may suffer a few trials at first, but when she marries the prince she lives happily ever after. I had only to be a good girl and everything would be all right.

The terrible blow about Danny had shaken this belief. I saw that maybe I was just an unimportant Ugly Sister. I wasn't safe anymore. My childlike faith evaporated, assisted by the fact that I had disobeyed the Church by going on the pill. My belief in God, which had been the central pivot of my life, left me. I was plunged back into the meaningless world I had inhabited before I was eight years old.

One night I had a nightmare where I dreamed that the universe was like a huge onion. Layer on layer was pulled away until there was nothing left, just blackness and a diabolical jeer: "Nothing. Nothing. Nothing."

I woke up in a dreadful sweat, feeling sick in the pit of my stomach. For a long time I battled with this inner torment. Then one night it reached a crisis. I heard the jeering again: "There is Nothing. Nothing."

I felt that this was true: I knew that there was no God. Then I heard a command deep inside me, "Jump and I'll catch you."

I felt as though I were on the edge of a precipice. Below me there was a pit of nothingness. I was sure that this was all there was. And yet I heard God calling me and telling me to jump. I was being asked to trust in someone who wasn't there.

I closed my eyes and jumped. And God caught me. Perhaps this was the only really free act I have ever made in my life.

What I saw then was that God who had caught me was suffering with me. He was not up in the sky judging like a stern grandfather, He was in me! Or rather, at my deepest point of suffering, I joined Him.

Since then, the trust that God is with me in any suffering that I may have to undergo has never left me. I was not immediately better. It was a long climb out of the mess I had got myself into. I had developed habits of self-pity and a morbid obsession with my internal state. But now I began to put up a fight.

One evening on the television I heard a psychologist say, "I am certain that anyone who really wishes not to be in a bad mental state can get rid of it." This may or may not be true, but it was what I needed to hear. I wondered if there was a secret wish in me to be insane, and then I saw that at the back of my mind lurked a picture of myself in a white bed, lying at peace while a white-coated doctor bent over me solicitously. I shuddered when I realised this and thought of what a real mental hospital would be like! Far from taking away my problem, I would be making it much worse.

I began to struggle against "wiggling my mind" like a tooth. I saw it was my duty to be cheerful and think positive thoughts and to pursue things that I enjoyed. I threw myself into my painting, and painted out all my morbid thoughts. My husband didn't like these pictures but I knew I needed to paint them.

One day at the surgery Dr. Sutton advised me not to do them, but to try painting flowers instead. I said to him, "How would you feel if you could never prescribe anything stronger than aspirin?"

Dr. Sutton was always honest. He said, "I would not be able to carry out my profession and life would lose much of its meaning."

Chapter Fifteen

Expansion

As I grew stronger, and Danny was settled and happy, the whole family began to expand in various ways. My sister Sheila and her husband Shane had moved to live near us some years earlier, and now they came regularly to lunch on Sundays. Sheila had produced three little girls in rapid succession, and Tommy especially enjoyed their company. As he was just two years older than Roisin, Sheila's oldest girl, he enjoyed being in charge of three younger children for a change.

At table Jim regaled us with stories about his job work-studying the refuse collectors. He worked with the men, doing a round with a different team each week. He told a story about collecting one dustbin when a man came storming out, complaining about rubbish that had been spilled the week before. When he saw Jim he halted and stared.

"Where did you get that tie?" he demanded. "That's a Trinity College graduate tie!"

"I am a graduate of Trinity College," said Jim, picking up the dustbin and carrying it out, leaving the man staring after him open-mouthed.

Jim said you could tell a lot about people's characters from looking at their dustbins. Paradoxically, the richer the person, the less waste. From the poorest areas the dustmen collected almost new furniture and bikes. Then they had to drive for miles up to a stately home just to empty one bin containing seven used tins of Kat-o-meat. There were many other such stories; Jim was always an amused observer of human nature.

After lunch Shane and Jim would talk over their school and college days while Sheila and I exchanged ideas on art over the washing up. She had started a nursery school as well and did portraits of the children there to earn extra money.

I enjoyed the leisurely Sunday lunches, but Jim and I had arguments over other callers. Jim knew many couples who liked to drop in without warning and spend hours talking about politics or cars. I wouldn't have minded if I could have gone on with my painting while they talked, but Jim said it was my duty to sit and listen. He had a thing about "the sacred laws of hospitality." I felt I had to obey him because I valued our marriage and I wanted the safety of his approval, but it was agony to sit there with my fingers itching. There were so many paintings to finish, and time was ebbing away.

It was a great disappointment to me that Jim took little interest in my art, and I learned to accept that he was not primarily a visual person. The look of his surroundings meant very little to him, but he was interested in music and encouraged the boys in their music lessons. Charlie learned to play the flute and Thomas had piano lessons, but Danny continued unmusical.

It was a triumph for me when my paintings began to sell and thereby I earned respect from Jim. This gave me confidence as well as enabling me to employ a woman to clean the house, which badly needed it.

I started a fund which I hoped one day would enable me to go to Vienna and study with the artist Ernst Fuchs, whose work I had seen in London a few years earlier. I longed to know how he had achieved such brilliant colours and transparent glazes. I wrote to my Mother when I heard that she and my Father were planning a visit to Vienna in the new year, and asked them if they could find this artist and ask if I could study with him.

Mother promised to do this, and I waited impatiently for the outcome. Meanwhile several people asked me if I would give them painting lessons. This was a success, and eventually I was given a job at West Herts College where I taught art classes two afternoons and two evenings a week.

Much as I liked teaching, I missed the contact with other serious artists that I'd had at art school. So one evening I went along to the Halstead Art Society.

To my disappointment it mainly consisted of respectable elderly ladies painting water-colours of flowers. However, I noticed two younger artists there and I was thinking of going over to talk to them, when a strange figure entered the room, and there was a shocked silence.

The new arrival looked like Rip van Winkle arriving back after his fifty-year sleep on the mountaintop. His hair and beard straggled down his front and back in wild disorder. His trousers were held up with rope, and two odd socks poked out of paint-bespattered sandals.

No one spoke to him, so after the meeting was over I went over and introduced myself. He said his name was Tristram, and he was a technician, but painted in his spare time. I invited him and the other two young artists, Jack and George, to my house for coffee, to meet Jim.

Over coffee we began to exchange ideas about art. We agreed that we weren't going to learn much from the Halstead Art Society. We had all been disappointed in it. However Jim suggested that it might be useful for us to continue as members because through the official society we had the chance of exhibiting locally and selling our work.

Jack said, "We could be a splinter group!" We agreed and decided to band together and experiment with different techniques of painting. In this way we would progress by learning from each other. I showed them the catalogue of the Vienna School of Fantastic Realism with the paintings of Ernst Fuchs, and we decided to try to discover for ourselves the techniques he was using.

I ran upstairs and brought out my old art books. There was a book on making gesso panels, which I'd always meant to do when I had the time. Tristram seized the book and scanned the pages intently. "I could get the materials," he said. "We could make the gesso boards at my house. Mother won't mind!"

We all responded with enthusiasm and planned to meet next Tuesday evening. Jack offered to collect George and me and drive us to Tristram's house.

None of us ever forgot that first visit. The house was set far back among dark trees. Jack parked the car and as we walked to the door we heard the gurgling sound of running water getting louder and louder.

We stood in front of the door and rang the bell. After awhile the door opened a crack, and a ghostly woman peered out. She had white hair and a deathly pale face. Even her eyes were pale grey. We asked for Tristram and she muttered something and tried to close the door, but then Tristram appeared and she scuttled away.

"Sorry, that was Mother," said Tristram. "She's not used to visitors." He led us up a broad staircase.

"What was that gurgling sound outside?" asked Jack.

"That? Oh, the tap leaks," said Tristram carelessly. He pointed to the bathroom and we peered inside to witness an awesome sight. The bath tap was pouring out water without ceasing, making the whole room glisten with dampness. High up in the corners of the ceiling strange growths had established themselves. They weren't just patches of fungus, they were long green and brown fronds swaying in the air, like the swamp trees in Louisiana. The bath was deeply stained in interesting patterns of brown and orange.

We gazed at it in awed silence. Then Jack asked, "How long has the tap been leaking?"

Tristram thought for a moment, "About seven years I think. But never mind that, come and see the attic."

We climbed another set of stairs and then Tristram cried, "Wait there!" He rushed up the attic stairs, and then we heard a rumble and through a hole that had been bashed into the wall of the stairwell, a little steam train came puffing out along a tiny track that had been laid above our heads, and it vanished into a hole bashed into the opposite wall.

We jumped in surprise, wiping off the hot water and oil that had dripped on to us, while Tristram's beaming face peered out from the attic door. "Did you like that?"

"Amazing!" I said. "My boys would love it!"

"Come up. Come up!" said Tristram. We climbed up and entered the attic room. It was a little boy's dream. There was a magnificent train set, complete with everything including stations, trees and little people. We all admired it, but Tristram looked preoccupied. After a while he said, "I'm going to get rid of it all."

We stared at him. "Yes," he said, "I'm going to turn this into a studio where we can make gesso boards and paint our pictures. This will be the meeting place for our new group."

Chapter Sixteen

The London Gallery

The next Tuesday meeting was a great success. Tristram had cleared the floor and made a wonderful place to work. There were cushioned benches to sit on, and a kettle and mugs all ready. Tristram suggested that we each choose a mug and stick to it every time as he didn't like washing up.

We all worked together intensively, preparing gesso panels and painting vigourously to the sounds of music, varied occasionally by odd recordings Tristram had made of bagpipes played by being connected to a vacuum cleaner, or the amplified sound of a snail eating cabbage.

To our surprise, Tristram had put a lock on the door, which he bolted when we were all inside.

We soon found out why. As the evening wore on we heard the handle of the door being tried several times. Then there was a knocking and a banging and a querulous voice calling, "Tristram! Tristram!"

"What is it, Mother?" he asked, his face like thunder.

"I've made your cocoa."

"Leave it on the step."

"But it will get cold!"

"I don't want it, now go away!" Out of kindness we talked loudly amongst ourselves, pretending not to hear.

One evening we arrived at the studio to find that Tristram had completed a painting. It was extraordinary. It showed a huge engine coming down the tracks. It was painted so that the front of the engine looked like a human face an exact replica of Tristram's mother. On the tracks in front of her was a tiny human being, about to be run over. He had Tristram's face. The whole effect was weirdly compelling.

I gazed at it in amazement, and realised that Tristram had a touch of genius. It was surprising to find such an artist in an inartistic town like Halstead, but here before me was the genuine thing.

Jack and George too were both talented and enthusiastic. My imagination leapt forward, picturing our small painting group expanding to become a great new movement in art, like the Impressionists. With my incurable imagination, I pictured our group appearing in art history books of the future!

After much discussion we decided to call ourselves the Inscape Group, after a word invented by Gerard Manley Hopkins. It was meant to convey the idea of an inner landscape, which was what our painting was about. As we discussed ideas and experimented with paints, we were filled with a sense of liberation. We felt free to paint anything we liked.

I realised then that up to now I had been painting in obedience to my mother. She had taught me her techniques and her ideas, but if my work were to be really mine I needed to find my own voice. I let go all my preconceived ideas, and splashed about with paint like a child playing in the mud.

Much as I loved my husband and children, it was ecstasy to go to the Tuesday painting meetings. At home I was wife, mother and housewife, but with the Inscape Group I could be myself. Sometimes on my way to the studio I would take great leaps in the air for pure joy. (When no one was looking!)

The Inscape Group flourished, and we began to show our work at the art exhibitions put on by the Halstead Art Society. They created a sensation. People didn't like them, but we felt we were the avant garde bringing modernism to the town.

As well as painting together, we began to meet socially. Jack's wife, Jill, was a great cook and gave wonderful parties, and the rest of us followed suit. At every party, during the course of the evening there would be a phone call. It was always for Tristram from his mother, saying his cocoa was ready or complaining that he had gone out without his scarf.

We incited Tristram to rebel. He was becoming more human, and he began to blossom and tell amusing stories which were even more unintentionally funny as they revealed aspects of his zany life.

Meanwhile our painting experiments on Tuesdays had resulted in a large number of works. While we hadn't discovered the technique of Ernst Fuchs, we had had a marvellous time dribbling enamel house paint onto gesso and swirling purple, orange and green oil paint over it to the sound of music. Tristram's studio floor was now coloured in a mess of epic proportions and was an artwork in itself.

One evening we lined up all the accumulated paintings against the wall and admired them. They represented hours of sheer enjoyment. I felt that now the time had come to let the world see our work. I said we must make an appointment with an art gallery in London. We browsed through a list of all the London galleries and I picked one with the most distinguished name: Roland, Browse and Delbanco. What could be more distinguished than that?

I telephoned in the morning to make an appointment for next Saturday and Jack drove us in. We arrived early for the appointment, but an assistant let us in and we spread our paintings out all along the walls of the gallery. I noticed that it was a very sparsely furnished grey room with only a few pencil drawings in it, so our work certainly brightened it up.

At last Mr. Delbanco emerged from upstairs, and we saw his pinstriped trousers descending the stairs. They reached the landing from where he could see our work, and they halted there and froze.

After a few moments I could bear the suspense no longer and rushed forward. "Tell us!" I begged. "Tell us what you think of our work!"

He gazed at us all through his monocle. He said, "I feel like a doctor fazed with a lot of hopeless cazes!" Then his face suddenly turned red with anger and he shouted, "Get out! Get out! Get these things out of my gallery!"

We were unceremoniously flung out into the street.

Chapter Seventeen

Back to the Drawing Board

We gathered up our work and loaded it into Jack's car, and he drove us back home in silence. No one spoke to me, but I knew they blamed me for this debacle. If I hadn't insisted on taking our work to London we would never have been insulted like this. There were no more meetings on Tuesday evenings for some time.

I was shattered. Not only did I feel responsible for letting the group in for this insult, but my belief in my own work was destroyed.

Jim kindly urged me to accept that I wasn't good enough and use my art as a hobby for my own amusement. But I couldn't do that. Either what I was doing had value, or it wasn't worth doing. I felt numbed, and unable to paint anymore. Now I could see that the exuberant work we had done on Tuesdays had been messy and self indulgent.

Then one evening I felt a little flame kindle inside me and the determination to fight back. "I will prove that dealer wrong," I thought. "I will work until my paintings *are* good!" I set myself the task of going back to drawing, and resolved to do a drawing from life every day. I made many pencil sketches of the children in action. This also had the effect of focussing my attention back on to them after my absorption in the world of art.

Danny enjoyed posing for me because he liked the attention. Since our trip to Zurich, he had become very gallant towards me. He called me his "bird". One day, however, I annoyed him and he told me to go away.

"I thought I was your bird!" I said, rather hurt.

"Well, fly away then," he responded.

One evening I was all dressed up for a party when I went to say good night to the children. When I went to Danny's room he gazed at me in admiration and said, "Mum, you should enter the Miss World competition, I'm sure you'd win!"

However, I was not his only sweetheart. One of my pupils, a retired school teacher called Dorothy England, had visited our house and met Danny, and taken him to her warm heart.

She invited him to visit her after Mass on Sunday. Danny prized these visits. It was an invitation only to him, not his brothers, and while he was there Dorothy gave him her full attention. She was a tall, handsome woman in her early sixties, full of intelligence and humour.

Danny was very fond of her and told her that if he were older he would have liked to marry her. This amused her, but she was touched all the same. When she told me afterwards about their conversations she was very concerned over his lack of self-esteem.

"He's always boasting about his brothers!" she said. "He never says anything about himself!"

Danny was devoted to his father. He saved his pocket-money for nearly a year, adding money he earned by doing little jobs around the house, so that at Christmas he could buy his father a "Teasmade"—a machine that combined a clock alarm with a kettle so that it woke you with a cup of tea.

His father was deeply touched by the gift. He said that in many ways he felt that Danny was closest to him in character. They both loved history, and Jim bought Danny serialised histories of both the First and Second World Wars that ran into many volumes and filled the entire top shelf of Danny's bookcase.

Charles was immersed in his research into science. I was impressed to see him cycle into town to the library in order to copy out all the atomic weights. It was funny when, late at night as I went the rounds, tucking up the children, Danny would have storybooks and Thomas would have toys, while Charles had nodded off over the Engineer's Handbook. As Charlie learned more, there were little explosions around the house, culminating at breakfast one morning when there was a big bang and splintering glass all over the toast. After that, Charlie's experiments were banned from the house and confined to the shed.

Tommy was a funny little boy. He came up to me one day and demanded, "What's the end of numbers?" "There isn't an end to numbers," I said, "because you can always add one more." Tommy didn't like that answer, and frowned. "There *must* be an end to numbers!" he insisted. "No," I replied. "There really isn't. No matter how big a number is, you can always add to it."

Tommy's face went bright red with fury and he began to hit me. "Say that there is an end to numbers!" he roared.

The fact that I had begun to laugh only made things worse, so finally I had to send him to his room for naughtiness. But in a funny way I knew why he was upset. It was like glimpsing eternity, very frightening.

Just after Christmas my mother arrived from Vienna on a visit to Sheila and me. She had brought a birthday present for me: an etching by Ernst Fuchs! She had tracked him down and visited his studio, and told him about my wish to study with him and he had asked me to write to him.

I was ecstatic! I hung up the etching in the living-room and sat down to write to Ernst Fuchs, dizzy with excitement.

He wrote back, asking for samples of my work. I sent all the photographs I possessed, and even included a small painting. He wrote back saying that my ideas and drawing ability were there, but that I lacked the right technique of painting for what I wanted to express. He said that although he did not usually take pupils, if I would come to Vienna he would teach me the technique he had evolved from the Renaissance school of painting.

How I yearned to go! It seemed the one thing I needed to progress in painting. But how could I get away?

I showed the letter to Jim. He said, "Why don't you go?"

I was startled. "But I couldn't! I could never leave the children, especially Danny!"

"Danny's fine now," he said. "If you can get someone to look after the children while I'm at work, I'll look after them at weekends." I was thrilled by his encouragement, and this gave me the incentive I needed.

Then everything fell into place, as if I had been meant to go. A sale of a painting raised the amount of my savings so I had enough to pay for the trip, and an artist friend was looking for an au pair job for two weeks. So she came to mind the children while I got ready to go to Vienna to study this magic new painting technique.

Chapter Eighteen

Ernst Fuchs

As I left for the airport I was very nervous. I was still dependent on tranquillisers and carried a supply in my handbag, taking an extra one whenever I felt stressed. I found a pension-hotel near the center of Vienna and dumped my luggage, then I set out with a map of the city to find Ernst Fuchs's studio.

I came to an imposing street lined with tall old buildings of carved stone. Inside one of these I entered a dark vaulted hall, where the stairs spiralled upwards. Fuchs lived at the top floor. Gasping for breath after the climb, I rang the bell. A jolly maid in an apron opened the door. She led me to a large studio filled with a golden light from the setting sun, where a man in an Oriental cap sat working. He looked up as I came in. I saw a beautiful face, very pale and finely chiselled, with dark hooded eyes and a black beard.

"So you are Brigid!" he greeted me with a smile. I was overwhelmed. All around me were paintings, some exquisitely beautiful, some horrific.

"I can't believe I'm here!" I said, and to my embarrassment two large tears jumped out and rolled down my cheeks. Ernst looked concerned and ordered me a coffee and sandwiches, which restored my equilibrium.

"Now we must arrange your plan of work," he said. "How long can you stay?"

"Two weeks. I couldn't leave the children for longer." He shook his head. "You make it very difficult for yourself. This is not an easy technique to learn."

"I'll work hard," I promised.

Next morning I arrived early as Ernst was having breakfast. "It's the early bird waiting for her worm!" he joked. When I opened my paint box he made a face at my filthy smock and chewed up paint tubes.

"You know," he said gently, "to be a great artist you must be like a chemist, everything should be spotless and in order!"

I looked up and saw his white overall and the perfectly arranged studio. I had thought that artists were always scruffy. Then and there I resolved to change my bad habits.

"I call this way of painting the Mische Technique," said Ernst. "It comes from the German word 'misch' meaning 'mixed'. In this technique we paint alternately with water- and with oil-based mediums."

I was given a gesso panel and I set to work on a self-portrait with peacock feathers. The board was given a coat of bright red, and then I had to paint over it with white egg tempera diluted with water. This was very hard to handle. My brush strokes looked rough beside his delicate ones. I had to do it over and over until I had mastered the right way of painting. At last I achieved a better result, and Ernst took me out for a coffee to celebrate. He asked about my family. I told him about Danny and all our problems with him, and I said it was sometimes hard to go on painting when my work didn't seem to be appreciated and when so many of my neighbours thought it was a useless occupation.

He stroked his beard. "It depends on what you call useful! All our writing originally derived from picture-making. Civilisations are characterised by their art. But I believe art can be more than that, it can be a prophecy, a message from a higher world. The artist can be the medium through which the message comes."

"Is this what we usually call inspiration?" I asked.

"Yes. Inspiration is being contacted by spirits. In fact, we are always being contacted by spirits, good and bad. If you do something by inspiration, you do it to a pattern which is pre-existent. Michelangelo expressed this when he said that the statue was always there he only helped to free it from the block of marble. The artist succeeds to a greater or lesser degree, according to his gift."

I felt supported by this talk. Ernst Fuchs's ideas were backed up by his own amazing work. But could I reach the same level of inspiration, and would I be able to learn this technique in this short time? I realised it was now or never. I had to prove myself as a painter. At home I was always being interrupted by household duties; here I had no excuse. If I couldn't produce a good painting under these circumstances, I would never produce one.

I began to see what I lacked: self-discipline. Suddenly I felt I must stop depending on tranquillisers, and at that moment I resolved to give them up for good. In the morning I set to work with a new energy. I learned how to put on oil glazes and more layers of egg tempera. I had never worked so hard in my life. It was as if the technique had the power to lift me beyond anything I had been able to do before.

In the evenings I would arrive at the pension-hotel and fling myself on the bed, exhausted and elated. One night as I lay there I got into a strange state. I started to pray and entered into a sort of ecstasy. I felt as if my spirit had escaped and was floating up to the ceiling. Then I begged to die and be taken up to God. Suddenly I heard a voice say, "You have to go back and get your body."

I looked down and saw my body lying there, an unknown quantity. The strange state left me and I fell asleep.

The days went by, until inevitably the last day came. I would be leaving on the following morning.

At last, after a long stretch of painting, I finished and stood back, surprised. The picture looked as if it had been done by magic, as if it had sprung up overnight! At that moment Ernst Fuchs came in and stood behind me. I waited, but he said nothing for a long time. Then I felt a hand on my shoulder.

"I congratulate you, Brigid, that is well done! I did not think that anyone could have done a painting in this technique in so short a time!"

I left the painting to dry overnight and returned next morning to collect it and say goodbye. Ernst Fuchs gave it to me with a surprise present. He had put it in a beautiful gold frame! It was hard to part from this man who had given me so much of his time and so much friendship. In return I resolved never to forget what I had learned from him.

Jim and the boys met me at the airport. Danny and Charlie seemed happy and composed but little Tommy burst into tears when he saw me—he was angry with me for going away. Now I was glad to settle down to the normal routine. There was so much to think over and work on.

Mrs. Watt was very interested in the fact that I had gone to learn a new painting technique.

"But you were already a good painter!" she exclaimed. "Didn't you find it difficult to forget what you knew?"

"Yes, it was difficult."

"Then why did you go to all the trouble of learning a new way of painting?"

I was puzzled. "But this is better!"

"I couldn't do that," she said. "I couldn't forget everything I had learned in the past and start all over again as you have done!"

I looked at her in surprise. My trip to Vienna had been a gift that would last me all my life; there was nothing praiseworthy about my acceptance of this gift, anymore than one would praise a thirsty man for drinking water. I then realised that people are truly different. What is easy for one is difficult for another.

Many times I had admired Mrs. Watt's patience, her ability to go over and over the same subject until she was sure Danny had understood it. This was something I never could have done. She gave Danny more than lessons; she gave him part of herself.

Chapter Nineteen

The Inscape Group

A few weeks after I returned from Vienna I called a special meeting of the Inscape Group and told them of my meeting with Ernst Fuchs. By now the incident with the London Art Gallery had lost its sting and had become a funny story instead, so I was forgiven. The others were very interested in what I had learned from Ernst Fuchs, and we decided to meet together again on Tuesdays and work hard to master and develop the technique I had been shown.

Now that we were more serious, real results began to emerge. Tristram's ideas had always been good, but with the new technique they acquired a discipline and became more convincing. I found that working with this technique gave me a structure that paradoxically allowed more scope for my imagination. The others, too, tried the technique, but they became deflected in various ways. George went off with a different crowd called the "heads." He wanted to get inspiration by taking drugs, but the rest of us didn't trust that way of being inspired. I remembered that Ernst Fuchs, who had experimented with drugs himself, had written that taking drugs to get inspiration was like climbing over a wall to steal something that you could earn by work on yourself.

In his place one of my young students called Steve sometimes joined us. He was a meticulous draughtsman with an unusual imagination, but he was hampered by having to earn his living by working in a factory.

Jack, on the other hand, had resolved to give up his job at the printers and become a full-time artist. This meant that he had to do the kind of paintings that would sell quickly, things like landscapes with windmills or seascapes with boats. He sold them by going from house to house, knocking on people's doors. He complained that this prevented him from giving the time to his "soul" painting, as he called it.

Diana, a sculptor, joined the Inscape Group. She was a small woman who did enormous sculptures rather like the ones on Easter Island. She had a great sense of fun, and I found it a relief to have another woman around to put the female point of view across, but with the demands of five children she couldn't always come.

When the others weren't there, Tristram and I had long conversations about inspiration and its source. We read poetry together to inspire us with ideas for painting.

One day when Danny was having a bad bout of fits, I asked Tristram, "Why do you think some children have to suffer? There must be some meaning to it all, but I can't find it."

Tristram squeezed my hand. "I don't know." he said, "I've never been able to figure it out. It's like that poem by Blake, 'Every day and every night, some are born to sweet delight, some are born to endless night.'"

That was too much; "Danny's life isn't endless night!" I said crossly.

As a way of mastering the Mische technique, I set out to paint a portrait of each of my sons in turn. Danny's portrait showed him in front of a poster of one of his macho comic book heroes, which contrasted with the vulnerability of the young boy's face. Danny enjoyed sitting, and he watched the progress of the painting with great interest.

Charles's portrait already showed the face of a scientist. At seven years old he made a wonderful machine with his Meccano set, which lit up and turned a windmill. A few days later I asked if he would show it to some of my friends, but he said he had dismantled it.

"Oh, why?" I asked, puzzled.

"Because once I saw it would work, I didn't need it anymore," he said. I saw then the difference between artists, who want to preserve their creations, and scientists, who only want to use their creations in the pursuit of knowledge.

On the other hand Charlie was very upset when one of his experiments wouldn't work. He was trying to make a speedometer for his bicycle out of parts of his Meccano set so he could record his speed as he cycled. Unfortunately the construction was so heavy it kept falling off his bike the moment he tried to go fast. He came inside in despair and flung himself on the sofa. I tried to comfort him and he said, "It's just as if someone took one of your paintings, Mom, and broke it and stamped on it."

When Gran came on a visit she admired the portraits of the two older boys but asked when Thomas's would be finished. I told her I was having a hard time; Tommy was the most difficult to paint. Capturing that energetic bundle and making it sit down quietly on a chair was almost impossible.

Then Thomas started school, and it gave me a pang to see that by now the policy had changed and mothers were allowed to come and settle their children in. What a difference that might have made to Danny! Whereas Tommy, after holding my hand tightly for a minute, found a friend and shouted, "You can go now, Mummy, I don't need you any more!"

I knew he enjoyed school because our house was near the playground and I could hear his voice at recess loudly organising all the games. He was a great sports enthusiast, devoted to football, and spent his life playing the game outside and even inside the house.

After school one evening Tommy told me about a little girl in school who was bad at everything. She couldn't read and she was very bad at games. "She is useless!" he said scornfully.

I said, "Tommy, everything we can do well is like a gift. You have been lucky, you have a lot of gifts. It's like at Christmas; if one child got a lot of presents and another child got no presents, should the lucky child jeer at the poor one?"

He didn't answer, but later at the School Sports Day when he won the race, I heard him turn and congratulate the others. "You did very well! You ran very fast! It was just luck that I beat you."

Tommy was always surrounded by a crowd of little boys. I could see Danny watching him with envy. During the holidays the house was filled with boys, surging around the place. It was difficult to concentrate on my painting, so sometimes I would get up and bellow at them all, chasing them out into the garden. As they went I heard Tommy explaining to his friends, "That's just Mum's artistic temper."

Meanwhile I was not progressing with Thomas's portrait. I sat him down and told him stories, then I bribed him with sweets, and finally I paid him. But at last he refused to sit at all, even when I offered to double his salary. Sadly I realised I would not be able to finish the picture.

Then one morning there was a crash and a football came sailing in through the window. Thomas had disobeyed orders about not kicking footballs near the house, a rule laid down by his father, who was tired of repairing windows. I charged down the street after him like an avenging angel, and he shouted over his shoulder as he fled, "I'll pose! I'll pose!"

So the portrait was finished after all.

Chapter Twenty

Danny Goes to School

One day Mrs. Watt said to me as she was leaving, "I think it is time that Danny went to school."

I felt quite faint. Couldn't Danny go on learning safely with her? But she shook her head. "He is nine years old now, he needs to meet boys of his own age, and to cope with the outside world. "

I could see the logic of this, but I remembered the horror of his last time at school, and was full of fears.

Miss Sandy, the educational psychologist who treated Danny with such thoughtfulness when he was six, came to visit and discuss the matter. She drove me to her house for tea. We passed the new park there, which had been planted with new trees, all marching like soldiers in exact rows.

"Don't they look awful!" I exclaimed. "Not like trees at all!" Miss Sandy gave a rueful smile, "I suppose that is what happens when we try to impose our sense of order on the world."

I was struck by this. "I suppose I want to impose my idea of order on the world too, like keeping Danny safe at home."

Miss Sandy shook her head. "It's important to know when to let go and move on to the next stage. Danny needs to grow and develop, and for that he needs boys of his own age."

"But he is so vulnerable!" I exclaimed, and told her how I had always felt that Danny had one skin less than other people. Miss Sandy seemed to understand just what I meant, and she agreed with me. "We must temper the wind to the shorn lamb," she said. "We will send him to a very special school."

She told me about a private boarding school called Westbrook, only three miles away. Danny would not board but go as a day-boy, and he would be in a class of only ten boys. The atmosphere was that of a large family and the surroundings in the country were beautiful. The place had once been a country house. I had heard of it, and knew how expensive it was.

"We couldn't afford the fees!" I said regretfully. Miss Sandy said that as Danny was a special case, the Herts County Council was prepared to pay his school fees, providing that we would pay for his transport. He would need a taxi to go there and back, as I couldn't drive.

By the time Miss Sandy brought me back home I had begun to be more hopeful about the idea. It would be marvellous if Danny could make the adjustment. Then he would be just like a normal boy! The school could give him his lunchtime pills, so they need not be a problem either. Jim was very pleased to hear that Danny was ready for school and said that paying for a taxi would not be a problem.

On the first day of school Danny went off proudly in a taxi. He was all kitted up in a splendid outfit that we'd had to buy in London at the John Lewis stores. He had outgrown his dislike of new clothes and loved the school outfit that proclaimed him to be a schoolboy like all the others. They were beautiful clothes; the blazer was wine-red with golden eagles embroidered on the pocket and the matching cap. The tie was striped red and gold.

I put him into the taxi and said goodbye, longing to go with him, but realising that this would make him look a sissy.

All day I watched the clock anxiously, waiting for his return. I needn't have worried. Danny came back glowing with happiness, delighted to be in a proper class with other boys.

Mrs. Watt had taught him so well at the end of the school term he carried off all the school prizes! Mrs. Watt remained a friend to all of us. Danny was always fond of her; after one visit he said in his newly acquired school drawl, "Good old Watters!"

He loved being just like the other boys. I would watch him assume a careless stance: one hand in his pocket, his legs crossed, he would loll against the wall in a lordly way. Under the careless manner you could see his exultation—he was a proper ordinary schoolboy at last!

We shared his exultation. We had proved the psychiatrists wrong, Danny was going to be fine. All that had been wrong with him, we reasoned, was a kind of pre-epileptic condition, a sort of disturbance while the epilepsy was emerging; now he was just a normal boy who happened to have epilepsy.

Miss Sandy came to see Danny and to share in our joy, but she brought sad news. She had come to say goodbye as she was going to live in Malta. I tried to look happy for her sake but underneath I felt deserted. Who could I turn to now if anything went wrong?

We joined the Epilepsy Society. I made friends with a woman of my age called Jennifer, who suffered from both epilepsy and diabetes. Her courage and intelligence became an inspiration to us all, especially Danny.

One of the things I enjoyed most was reading out to the children in the evenings. It had begun with nursery rhymes when they were very young and progressed to children's books. When they were smaller, Charles and Danny loved

Thomas the Tank Engine, but Tommy and I preferred Winnie-the-Pooh.

One night I was reading the last chapter, when Christopher Robin says goodbye to his toy animals because he is growing too old for them. Ridiculously, I became caught up in the pathos of the toys being left behind, and my voice became a little unsteady. I felt Tommy's comforting arm around me, "Don't cry, Mum, I still love my koala bear."

As the children grew we moved on to more exciting books and eventually we read Tolkien's *The Lord of the Rings*. Danny's eyes shone as I read, and when we got to a powerful moment, he exclaimed, "It's very dramatic, isn't it, Mum!"

That spring it was time for Danny and Charles to make their Confirmation. I decided to borrow some catechism books from the local Catholic School in order to instruct the boys. The books were not a success. For example, one lesson entitled "Christ as King" suggested that the teacher ask the pupils to name qualities that they would look for in a leader, and then go on to show those qualities in Christ.

However when I asked Danny what qualities he would look for in a leader he said promptly, "Wickedness!"

"Wickedness?" I repeated, puzzled, "in a leader?"

"Yes," Danny answered calmly, "Ghengis Khan, Hitler, Stalin ..." I put the catechisms away and went back to my home-grown methods.

On the day of the Confirmation the Bishop presided over the ceremony. He asked questions in church, telling the children to raise their hands if they wanted to answer, and I was bursting with pride to see Danny's crimson blazered arm and Charlie's purple one waving in the air. They answered the questions correctly though they hadn't gone to the parochial school.

One night when Danny was having a fit in bed—they often came at bedtime—I said to him, "I am so sorry for you, Danny." He answered, "Don't be sorry for me, be sorry for Jennifer. She is epileptic and diabetic."

I told this to Father Foster as an example of Danny's unselfishness, and he said, "Yes, but maybe he doesn't want people to be sorry for him. None of us wants that, do we?"

Only one small thing bothered me occasionally, a feeling that Danny was acting like a robot. It was as if he had programmed himself to appear normal, and all his gestures and mannerisms seemed a part that he had learned with great effort. But it was easy to brush those misgivings aside. Danny did act spontaneously from time to time, but then his behaviour was slightly odd.

One afternoon when Danny had arrived home early from school I was having a tea party with friends, and he offered to make the tea for us. I was very proud of him, he looked so handsome in his uniform, and he knew that he was at a "posh" school and enjoyed the kudos. I was delighted at the chance of showing him off to my friends.

In a short while Danny arrived back with a loaded tray. The tea was a bit weak, but we drank it down while Danny watched us with interest.

"Did you like the tea?" he asked solicitously. There was a polite murmur of assent.

Danny grinned, "I made it with the economical tea bags." he said.

I was puzzled. "The economical tea bags? What are those?" Danny beamed. "I saved up all the old tea bags and dried them, and now I used them again."

Around this time my youngest sister Liz came to London to study medicine. During her holidays she visited Sheila and me, and then history repeated itself. She fell in love with Shane's friend Cliff, they married, and when Liz qualified they moved out near Sheila and me.

All this time I had been corresponding with Ernst Fuchs, and now he wrote that he had set up an art gallery in Vienna and invited me to exhibit there. I sent off samples of my recent work and that of the other members of the Inscape Group. Ernst chose Tristram's work as well as mine. We were very excited and worked hard to get enough paintings for the show.

Sometimes as we worked together, Tristram began to confide in me. He said how lonely he felt and how much he would like to be married, but no girl would ever look at him. Gently I suggested that perhaps he would find someone if he redesigned himself. He stared at me in surprise. "But surely people don't judge other people by their appearances!" he said. "It's what's inside that counts."

"That's true," I agreed, "but they will never get to the inside if they are put off by the outside."

"What do you mean?" he asked.

"Well, would you be interested in a girl that looked like this?" I mussed up my hair, put paint on my glasses and put on one of his filthy old smocks. He looked thoughtful, but said nothing.

Tristram and I exhibited our new paintings in the Mische technique at the next art exhibition in Halstead. When I arrived at the opening evening our pictures were attracting a great deal of interest. Different artists came up to ask me how we had achieved these unusual effects, and I was beginning to tell them about Ernst Fuchs when my mouth dropped open in surprise.

Just coming through the door I saw a transformed Tristram. He had on a new suit, he wore new shoes and his hair and beard were nicely styled. For the first time you could see that he was really handsome! He came up with a big grin to be admired, and I told him he looked marvellous! However, I didn't have him to myself for long soon he was surrounded by admiring women.

I felt a sudden pang. Something told me it would not be long before I lost my painting pal.

One Tuesday evening a few months later Tristram shyly told us that he was engaged to be married. Her name was Marian. The wedding would take place soon after he returned from taking our work to the show in Vienna, and we were all invited.

On the following Tuesday there was a strange silence as we drove up to the house; the sound of the gurgling waterfall had gone. Inside, the house was undergoing a transformation. The bathroom had been cleaned and pots of house paint lay about everywhere.

That evening turned out to be the last Inscape meeting at Tristram's house. There was no rattling at the door handle and no cocoa waiting on the steps outside, and we were puzzled and discreetly asked after his mother. He told us that Marian and his mother had not got on, and his mother had been very upset and had decided to go up north to live with her sister.

He looked a little embarrassed and said that Marian wanted the attic for storing things so the Inscape Group would have to find another meeting place.

We left in a subdued manner. It was lovely for Tristram that he had found happiness, but the rest of us mourned the end of the Inscape meetings as we had known them.

"I even miss the leaking tap!" Jack confessed.

Meanwhile Alison, an old school friend from Canada, wrote to me saying she was very unhappy. She had a severely handicapped child. I advised her to come and live in England. She moved to London and found a place for her child to be cared for. When I visited her she told me she had been through a messy divorce, and she looked thin and shaken.

Overcome with pity, I invited her to come and stay with us to recover. As I did so, into my mind flashed a story I'd read in a magazine, warning wives not to invite their divorced girlfriends home as this had broken up many marriages. But I pushed the thought away. What would life be if we couldn't trust one another?

So Alison came to visit, and she spent a lot of time asking Jim's advice on her financial problems. She asked him if he would visit her in London and help her sort them out. By the end of her stay with us she looked a lot better, and I was pleased that we'd helped her get over her divorce.

Chapter Twenty-one

Mother's Visit

Jim was so good at his job that he was promoted. Now that he had more time he followed up his interest in politics and joined the local Labour party. It wasn't long before he was made a Town Counsellor. People constantly sought his advice, and he went out of his way to help them. The phone was always busy as the local inhabitants regularly phoned him up to complain about the roads, rates, and annoying neighbours.

When the local elections took place, our house was used as area headquarters. Large red Labour Party posters were stuck in all the windows of our house, which stood conspicuously on the corner of the road. Then Jim called me outside in great embarrassment:

"Look what Danny has done. Can't you talk him out of it?" I went outside and started to laugh. There in the midst of all the red posters was a lone blue Conservative poster hanging from Danny's bedroom window. I talked to Danny and Jim argued with him in vain. Now that Danny attended a private school, he had taken on their politics. His father, believing as he did in the freedom of the individual, was forced to leave the poster there, where it hung defiantly all through the elections.

Now my mother came to visit her three daughters in turn. While she was with us I gave Danny his morning pills, and then he took an additional dose by mistake. I telephoned the doctor to ask what we should do, and he told us to keep

Danny in bed for the morning. It was a Sunday and Danny had planned to visit his friend Dorothy. I explained to him what the doctor had said and we decided he had better not go.

Danny received the news in stony silence. I was downstairs preparing lunch when I heard a great commotion in his room and rushed up, thinking Danny was having a grand mal fit.

He was standing in the middle of his room. He had poured all his pills on the ground and was smashing them with his feet in a rage.

"What are you doing?" I cried in horror.

"I'm *sick* of being epileptic!" Danny shouted. "I'm *tired* of taking pills! I'm not going to take them anymore!" He began to cry. "It's not fair!" he said, "Thomas isn't epileptic!"

"I know it isn't fair," I said. I put my arm around him and we sat on the bed and wept together.

Mother in the next room had heard him. She went out and came back half an hour later and called me into the living room.

Around her were stacks of envelopes and small toys and sweets. Beside her were a pile of envelopes with dates written on them. "I thought it over," she said, "and I realised that Danny needs a lot of little treats. If he has a present every time he must take his pills, it will give him a pleasant feeling instead of an unpleasant one. I've bought enough envelopes to last him three months. By marking the date and putting morning, noon, or evening on each one, you can see at once if Danny has taken his pills or not."

I sat down by Mother and helped her prepare the envelopes. Into each one we put a present. Some had just a little sweet, others had little books or toys. Every Sunday there was a special present for his noonday pills.

I went up to Danny's room and scooped up all the pills on the floor. Luckily most of them were undamaged and we could fill the envelopes with them.

Then I took the envelopes up to Danny. I put them in the top drawer of his bedside table and showed him what they were. Outside the door his two younger brothers looked on enviously. They had seen the envelopes being filled downstairs.

Danny's face shone with happiness as he fingered the envelopes. "I don't mind being epileptic anymore!" he said.

Mother's envelope system worked beautifully. Never again did we wonder whether Danny had taken his pills or not. As my mother remarked, the system worked because Danny was a patient and methodical boy. Another child might have ripped open the envelopes to get the presents earlier, but Danny never did.

Charles continued to be totally absorbed in science. It was interesting to see his steady pursuit of knowledge as he moved from chemistry, where there were explosions around the house and garden, to electronics, where I was scolded if one of his tiny bits was devoured by the hoover, to computers, where he started inventing a program to teach the computer to play Monopoly. One day we had a phone call from the school. Charles was in trouble. He had found a way in to the central computer in Hatfield and was tampering with the system there. He was only allowed back on the computer on the promise of good behaviour.

Tommy was due to make his First Communion, and I set about instructing him. It was difficult to focus his mind on anything but football. He kept asking me which football team I supported. I told him I wasn't interested in football, so I didn't support any team. Tommy was annoyed. "If you won't like football," he cried indignantly, "then I won't believe in fairies!"

I hadn't realised Tommy had taken the stories of my fairyfied childhood so seriously, but after that threat I tried to be more supportive, going to one of his school games and "supporting" a team. I chose Chelsea, because of the pretty blue shirts.

After Tommy's First Communion he was supposed to go to Mass on Sundays, but when he was picked for a team, the matches were played on Sunday morning at the same time as Mass. There was a service in the evening, but by that time he was tired and didn't want to go. For a while there were arguments, but then suddenly Tommy changed. He set his alarm clock, got up at seven-thirty in the morning and went to early Mass so as to be back in time for his match. I was surprised and pleased and I told him so.

He said, "Well, you see, Mum, I realised I was making a false god of football."

It was easy to see why he had been tempted to worship the game. Through his skill at it he had become a local hero. He was always surrounded by hordes of admiring friends. Danny watched him with envy. He longed to be like him and couldn't help being jealous, yet it was touching to see how much pleasure he derived from Tommy's triumphs. When Danny was celebrating his eleventh birthday, I asked him if he would like to invite some school friends to his birthday party. Danny shook his head. "I'll just invite Dorothy," he said. "Don't you want any of your friends from school, then?"

Danny shook his head. "I'm a lonely chap," he said. "I don't have many friends. I'd just like Dorothy."

Dorothy came and we had a merry party, but Danny's words grieved me. I had pictured him as being happy at school.

Later I received another shock. I was tidying up Danny's room when I saw a scrap book in which Danny was keeping newspaper clippings. When I opened the book and looked at the clippings I froze. Danny had cut out reports of murder, stabbing and violence, and stuck them in his book. I put the book back where he left it. I couldn't understand why he wanted to collect those things but I didn't feel I could question him about it. Danny had a right to privacy, too.

From time to time I noticed other oddities in Danny's behaviour. They were difficult to pinpoint but they all had to do with his inability to see another person's point of view. If anyone annoyed him or got in his way, he became hostile, whatever the circumstances. This caused friction between him and his brothers, and I could never reason him out of it.

On the radio I heard a talk about autistic children which disturbed me. The psychiatrists were explaining what autism was. They described an experiment that had been carried out involving three sets of children: normal children, Down's syndrome children and autistic children.

They put on a little puppet drama for the children. One puppet, Mary, has a bar of chocolate. Another puppet, Kate, comes into the room and sees the chocolate. When Kate isn't looking, Mary hides the chocolate under a cushion on a chair. Mary goes out, and Kate hunts around until she finds the chocolate under the cushion. She hides it in the wardrobe.

When Mary comes back, the children were asked, "Where does Mary think her chocolate is?"

The normal children answered immediately that Mary would think her chocolate was under the cushion. Even the Down's syndrome children, though it took them more time, could work it out. But the autistic children always answered that Mary thought her chocolate was in the wardrobe. They could not make the imaginative leap between what they knew to be true and what Mary thought was true.

This program left me in an uneasy depressed state. Yet I could not accept that there was anything else wrong with Danny but epilepsy.

Meanwhile, the exhibition in Vienna had gone well and a Paris dealer had invited me to exhibit my work at his gallery on the Left Bank. I was dazzled by this invitation and worked hard to produce more paintings.

But my exultation was short lived. One evening Jim told me that Alison had fallen in love with him and wanted him to leave his family and live with her. He promised that he would not leave us, but it was a terrible shock to me. I realised that it was my fault as well.

Because Jim had represented my bedrock of security I had taken him for granted, the way you take your parents for granted. Now my secure world was crumbling. I had been so absorbed by my painting and so interested in Tristram and the Inscape Group that I had not considered how Jim might be feeling. How blind I had been!

I went over and over the past in my mind, trying to change the way things had gone. There was such fear and confusion inside me that I felt I was on a carousel and couldn't get off!

Chapter Twenty-two

Kuwait

In my anxiety to find some basis for security, I began to read philosophical and spiritual books. My mother and I had long discussions by post. I found that there were excellent teachings in other faiths, and my mother agreed, writing, "After all, God isn't a Catholic!"

I was surprised. All the nuns in the convent schools I'd been to had led me to believe that He was!

Mother enjoyed our discussions, but after one visit she wrote to my father that when I prepared the meals she kept finding little "Teilhard de Chardins" in the salad.

Jim got fed up with my musings and asked, "Can't you stop thinking?" I thought it over for a long time but eventually had to admit that I couldn't.

One night, quite late, just before we were going to go to bed, little eight-year-old Thomas appeared in his pyjamas. His face was flushed and his eyes staring. "What's the matter?" we asked, surprised.

Tommy said, "I was lying there in bed and then all of a sudden I thought I wasn't there!" I took him up to comfort him, but Jim groaned, "Oh no! Not another ruddy philosopher in the family!"

Now Jim was appointed to a job abroad for six months; he had been so successful in reorganising the town facilities in Halstead that they asked him to do the same in Kuwait. He planned that he would go out for two months and then the three boys and I would go out for six weeks in the summer for a holiday. Then in a few more weeks he would be back.

Jim's absence brought some problems. Danny became more difficult when his father was away. He was twelve years old now and approaching puberty. I saw that he was testing me to see how far he could go in defying my authority. I avoided a confrontation for as long as I could, but one evening I was forced to take him in hand.

He had been watching television all afternoon and finally the two younger boys asked if they could watch a program on the other channel. I agreed, and Danny was angry. He went up to his room and came down with his cricket bat, threatening to assault his brothers with it. I demanded that he give me the bat, and then he threatened me with it. It was a frightening moment. I knew that he was quite a strong twelve-year-old and was nearly as tall as I was.

I had to act quickly and with authority, or there would be no dealing with him in the future.

I told him calmly that I would call the police, and they would come and take the bat away, and then I would send back the television so there would be no more fighting about it. I pointed out that it would save us a lot of money, not to have to pay the rent for the television every month.

Danny was the one in the house who liked television the most. He knew that my threat was not an idle one; I would be very pleased to have the television out of the house. He went upstairs meekly and put away his bat. I could even feel that he was relieved that I had won the battle; he had needed to test me, and he had needed to lose. That way he felt more secure.

One of the difficulties of dealing with Danny was that you never knew whether a problem came from a reaction to the pills he was taking or was due to any mental problems or was simply the onset of adolescence.

When the school holidays arrived we all flew out to Kuwait for the summer. It was very hot—the temperature went up to 140 degrees Fahrenheit—but everywhere indoors was air conditioned so it was bearable. When we went swimming we had to wear flip-flops right up to the water's edge, as the sand would burn your feet. On the horizon of the ocean were huge oil tankers, coming and going, and on the sand were gobbets of black oil that ruined all the swimsuits.

Luckily we stayed at a nice motel with a swimming pool near our rooms. I found Jim was cold and distant with me. He couldn't help showing his displeasure that I had been so neglectful of him in the past.

Sometimes other families with children would join us. One evening we were having a meal with another family when Jim made a disparaging remark about me. Then Danny spoke up. "Dad," he said. Jim turned to him. He was always very gentle with Danny.

"Yes?"

Danny said, "Mum's all right, Dad." Jim said nothing, but he changed the subject and stopped his criticisms.

The big event every week was the bingo game. People would travel miles to attend. It was a strange sight to see the sheikhs arrive with their wives in black burquas. Each sheikh would buy one card each for his wives and ten cards for himself, so that every time a number was called he would have the pleasure of filling a space.

Oddly enough, Danny was extraordinarily lucky. Time after time he would win, while the rest of us never won anything. He was very generous, however, and bestowed the gifts he'd won on us all: a set of matching towels for the house, a party dress for me and a giant bottle of perfume. He also won a lot of money. With this he went on a special shopping trip to buy a gold necklace for Dorothy.

The Arabs were very impressed with Danny's luck. The women would rush up to him to get him to touch their cards, or they would give Danny the money to buy their cards for them, hoping to fool the luck this way. Danny took it all in his stride, even when the women held up the cards for him to bless, which he did without any embarrassment.

When the children were in bed Jim and I had several long discussions. We had married young and were developing in different directions, but we both wanted to work on rebuilding our marriage.

When Jim finally returned from Kuwait, we made a new effort to live together in harmony. We tried to conceal our marital problems from the children, but one day Danny appeared with a quiz that he had cut out of a magazine. It asked questions like, "Are you pleased to see your husband coming home at the end of the day?"

I answered the quiz for Danny and he totted up my score. Then he cried, "Hurrah! That is over 80%. That means you won't get a divorce!" He rolled over on the living room carpet out of sheer joy.

I was flabbergasted. So Danny had been worried all this time! I felt ashamed that we two healthy people could not conduct our lives in peace, to give Danny the stability he needed. Of course, with his sensitivity he had known intuitively that something was wrong between us.

One evening Jim told me that he had tried to end his relationship with Alison, but she had threatened to kill herself, so he was still seeing her. I became very jealous.

Chapter Twenty-three

A Discussion Group

One night I had a dream. I was standing on the ground looking up at the sky. A pilot was flying a crystal aeroplane towards the sun. "He is flying too high!" voices cried all around me; "he will crash!" Then I realised that the pilot was me, and that I was in great danger. Suddenly there was a crash! The plane fell to the ground and shattered into a million pieces. My life was ebbing away. There was not a moment to lose.

I knew that I must telephone Miss Sandy; she was the only one who could help. I rushed to the telephone, but the round dial became a square and wouldn't turn. I woke up in a heavy depression.

That morning the phone rang. It was Miss Sandy! She had phoned to say she had come back to England to live.

When I heard her voice the dream came flooding back. In a wave of relief I cried, "I've had a dream! I must see you!" She did not seem surprised at my outburst. Instead she said she would like painting lessons.

She came over and we had a talk. We agreed to swap skills. I would teach her painting if she would help me. I told her about all my problems, how I had neglected my marriage, and how I now feared Jim would leave us. I felt I couldn't depend on him anymore, and it felt as though I were drowning in quicksand.

"I need to find some firm ground to stand on!" I said.

She answered, "There is a way of developing a firm ground in oneself, but it takes a long time and hard work to establish."

I wanted very much to find the firm ground. At first I thought that telling all my dreams would be the way forward towards learning, but then I saw Miss Sandy concealing a yawn. How could I find what I needed, then?

It was as if she knew, but she was very guarded. On her next visit some hippie artists dropped in. They were excited about the new "consciousness" that they had achieved and the seven chakras they worked with. One of them chanted dreamily, "How do you kill a dream tiger?" and the other answered, "With a dream sword!" Miss Sandy's voice cut through the miasma, "The way to kill a dream tiger is to wake up!"

I sat up, pierced by her voice.

"How do you wake up?" I asked when the hippie friends had floated off. She hesitated and then said, "Try watching yourself as if you were watching a film; try to see yourself as if you were another person, without wanting to change anything—just observe without praise or blame."

She left, and during the week I tried this, and became very uncomfortable. When Miss Sandy returned I told her that I had done what she suggested. "Did you notice anything?" she asked.

"Yes. I saw that I was totally self-absorbed. It was horrible!" Her eyes gleamed. "Without praise or blame!" she reminded me.

As I went on looking I saw more. How I wanted "Brigid" to get attention and be admired, how I brooded if "Brigid" was slighted. It was as if I had made an idol of myself, like a doll, that had to be worshipped. This had been going on all the time and I had never seen it! As I saw more, I began to have strange dreams; in one dream I was in bed with rats, in another I was in a very shaky house. I told Miss Sandy these dreams (but no longer in such detail!) and she said, "Dreams like these show us our inner state."

"My inner state! Surely I'm not that bad!"

"We all have many states in us," she said. "Each one of us is a universe. There are beautiful high mountains in us and also slums. We can live all our lives in our slums without realising it." I stared at her, still unconvinced. "For example," she went on, "sometimes if I am listening to the news, I can catch myself in a moment of pleasure when I hear that someone has been killed. That is the slum in me."

I was shocked. I didn't believe Miss Sandy would be pleased at anyone's death; I didn't think I had thoughts like that either.

But I did begin to see that it was my self-love that was bringing me the terrible pangs of jealousy. I needed help to control my emotions. Although Jim was visiting Alison he said it was just a friendship, that she needed him. I didn't believe in divorce, and the boys needed their father.

I thought it over. If I removed my own feelings from the situation, what was actually happening? Jim was a good father to the boys. They were not suffering. We all had enough to eat and to live comfortably. If I could remove my own ego, no one else need suffer.

But how could I deal with my overwhelming emotion? It was so strong it could poison my whole life.

When Miss Sandy came again to see me, I asked her in despair to help me. She calmed me down and sat quietly next to me. She asked me if I sincerely wanted to develop myself. I said I did.

"Well," she said, "I will give you an illustration of how to work on your jealousy, and you must find out for yourself if it is helpful. At the moment your jealousy is a very strong force it is almost like a rogue elephant running amok, isn't it?"

I nodded.

"The only way to control this rogue elephant is to bring two other elephants to either side of it; then it can be controlled. The two other elephants are the intellect and the body. You can use your mind and your body to help you with your emotions."

"But how?" I asked.

Miss Sandy shook her head reproachfully. "Think. Use your imagination and your intelligence. You have plenty of both." With an encouraging smile she left me.

I sat for a long time thinking over her words. It was true, my jealousy was indeed like a raging wild elephant. But how could I bring in my body and my mind?

The next time that I felt my emotions beginning to overpower me, I remembered Miss Sandy's words. I went out and began to mow the lawn. Something eased in me, but my thoughts still revolved endlessly in imaginary emotional arguments. I began to recite poetry as I mowed, and there was no room for the thoughts anymore. I began to feel clean and calm. To my surprise and joy, by working in this way the jealousy began to fade, but if I ever made the mistake of thinking it was completely gone, a moment's twinge would show me that I needed to continue the struggle.

Then one night I had a different dream. It began like one of my recurring nightmares where I was at the top of an enormous slope. I was in a car that was careering down the hill out of control. "I can't drive! I can't drive!" I cried in panic. Then the realisation came, "I can steer." I grasped the steering wheel and steered myself safely to the bottom of the slope. I woke up with a new sense of power; I had begun to be in control.

"This is amazing!" I told Miss Sandy. She nodded, "Yes, but you will find that this method does not work forever. After a while it will go stale and no longer be effectual. You have to renew something."

"Yes, but how?"

"It is to do with levels. We tend to take everything on one level, but there are different levels of being." She thought for a moment. "For example, I remember a toy I used to love as a child, a binocular which had slides of various scenes. When you put in two slides of the same scene, the two dimensional photograph became three dimensional."

I said, "Yes! I had one of those."

"Well, in the ordinary way we tend to be two dimensional, just mechanically going about our tasks. But if we were to bring another viewpoint into being, life could have more depth. There is a saying, 'As above, so below'. As we go deeper into our being, we become more aware of a higher level. It is from a higher level that we can receive help."

I must have looked as bewildered as I felt, for she laughed. "Perhaps you would like to read some books that would explain all this better than I can." She suggested *In Search of the Miraculous* by P. D. Ouspensky, and that afternoon I borrowed it from the library.

I read that there was a system of self-study based on the methods of spiritual development in the East, which had been brought to the West by a man called G. I. Gurdjieff. He was born in 1877 in Alexandropol and trained as a physician and priest.

Later I read Gurdjieff's own book, *Meetings with Remarkable Men*, which relates how he and a few companions, calling themselves Seekers of Truth, began to travel and search in the East. They found authentic ancient schools of knowledge and incorporated them in the living teaching that Gurdjieff brought back a system which has been called the psychology of man's possible evolution.

It was extraordinary to read of all the possibilities in a human being. It appeared that most of us live only in a tiny part of ourselves, as if we each owned a great mansion with many beautiful rooms but elected to live only in a small basement room. To develop we would need to find access to these other rooms.

Gurdjieff said that one of the aims of his system was to enable people to really live their faith. As a Christian I had struggled in vain to love my enemies as Christ had taught, but when I was in an irritable mood I couldn't even love my friends!

When I had read several books I said to Miss Sandy, "There are so many things I want explained!" She hesitated. "I am not a teacher, but I can put you in touch with someone who is more qualified. There have always been schools where people can be taught the way to self-knowledge. Every real religion has an inner core of such people. What one needs to avoid are fanatics and false teachers who set themselves up to be worshipped. A real teacher is there for a time to help you find your own inner voice. Perhaps there would be others studying with you, and what each one discovered could help the others."

I was anxious to be put in touch with a group like that. I begged Miss Sandy to give me the name of a teacher. She shook her head. "You are not yet ready for that. But if you like, we could form a discussion group."

I was pleased at this idea as several of my friends had shown an interest in similar questions. I had shown the books to Father Foster, who read them with great interest and suggested we hold the discussion groups in the presbytery, as he would also like to be there.

After one of the meetings he remarked, "You know, much of what is spoken of here is in the Philokalia, a book of instruction to monks in the early church. We have lost something that was once part of our religion."

After several meetings, Father Foster told us that he would soon be leaving the parish to work in London. We were very sad to think that we were losing him. With his departure the discussion group came to an end.

Again I begged Miss Sandy to put me in touch with a teacher, and this time she handed me a piece of paper with a name which I will call Dr. A. on it, and an address in Hampstead. She said that I could write to him saying why I wanted to join and what I hoped to receive.

I thought hard. How could I put what I hoped to receive into words? The only way would be to put down what I had already received. I did this as well as I could, and in a few days I received an answer. One of the other members of our discussion group, a woman called Dolores, had also written and received a reply. We were both invited to meet Dr. A. in Hampstead one Saturday morning.

Dolores and I discussed it many times together over endless cups of tea. We were suddenly nervous about the whole thing. All the things that we had read about weird fanatical groups and strange Eastern religions made us scared of what we might be letting ourselves in for. It was unknown and dangerous, but if we chose the safety of retreat we might never be given another chance. In the end we both found ourselves at the door in Hampstead at the appointed time.

Chapter Twenty-four

Dr. A.

The face of the man who opened the door was not that of a fanatic. It was a fully human face, marked by humour and suffering. He was a tall man in his seventies. He showed us into a spacious living-room, and as we sat down I noticed a piece of knitting on the table. Some impulse made me want to tease him so I said cheekily, "I didn't know you could knit!"

"It's my wife's," he answered, and then checked himself and gave me a shrewd glance. He saw what I'd been at, and repaid me in due course with his own brand of testing.

We all talked together but nothing was resolved. He merely said that we could telephone again in a month's time. I was determined to keep asking until I was admitted to his teaching; I kept on bringing the subject back to what I wanted until his eyes flashed at me.

"You are very greedy, aren't you!" he said.

I fell silent and we left soon afterwards. Dolores was indignant for me, but I couldn't speak. I felt as if a surgeon had finally put his finger on the diseased spot that had been troubling me for years. I felt relieved and frightened at the same time, together with a great joy because I felt that with him I would be in the right hands. In a flash I had seen that greed was a driving force behind all my wishes: I was greedy for fame, for affection, and now, even greedy for self-perfection!

I found it difficult to explain this to Dolores. She had been put off by his speaking to me like that. She wondered if after all this system of self-study was going to work for her.

We went to Hampstead again a few times; then one morning I overslept and missed the train! I caught the next one and thought, I must not be late or I may lose my chance. I counted the money in my purse there was just enough for a taxi to Dr. A.'s house. I arrived just at the appointed time.

"Is Dolores here?" I asked. We usually arrived a little early.

"No," Dr. A. replied.

I was astonished. "But she caught the train and I missed it! I had to come by taxi!"

A strange expression crossed his face, but he made no comment. We went into the living-room. Now that we were alone together, everything changed. Up to now I had been trying to appear sophisticated and wise, hoping to impress him. Now I felt that I could open up and tell him all my difficulties, and he listened with a look of boundless compassion. Then he said, "What do you want?"

"Oh! I want … to be a better person ... to serve God."

"What do you mean by that?"

"Well … whatever is good and ... true!"

He stared at me in astonishment. "But you are a child!" he said. It was a relief to drop all my pretences. "Of course I am." I had a fatherly smile as a reward, and then he said gently, "Yes, what you wish is what we all wish for, but that is very far from us as we are now. You need a smaller aim to start with."

I said, "I've been trying to sit still and meditate every day."

"And what did you find?"

I wanted to show off and say that I had found a deep inner peace, but instead I confessed the truth. "I found that I couldn't stop the noise going on inside me. There was a kind of talking going on the whole time." He smiled, and I felt that he was pleased because I had told the truth. He told me to stop trying to meditate for the time being.

"But I must!" I cried. "Otherwise life has no meaning!" I told him how I sometimes felt I was on a carousel and couldn't get off. He nodded, "Yet at the center of the carousel there is a part which is steady and still."

Then he said, "There is a way to find quiet. There is a right way." He gave me instructions which helped me a great deal, and showed me how the body can help the spirit. "We need our bodies," Dr. A. told me.

Then I told him about the strange experience I had gone through in Vienna, when my spirit had wanted to soar upwards and I had been told to go back and get my body. He was very amused by this, and then leaned forward and tapped me on the hand, saying, "And you and I know that this is true!" Then he looked at me very seriously and said, "Our group meets here on a Thursday evening at eight o'clock, can you make the journey every week?"

My heart leapt, then sank. "Of course I can make the journey. I'd love to join. It is only that I teach an art class on Thursday evenings." He gave me a probing look and said, "Sometimes there is a moment in life when a choice has to be made."

I went home thoughtfully. The next day I telephoned Mr. Owen, the man in charge of the classes, and asked if I could discuss something with him. The fact was that over the years I had infringed petty rules, and we had become arch-enemies.

What would happen now that I was going to break my contract in mid-term by dropping the Thursday evening class? At last he would have a real grievance. He could take all my other painting classes away from me, and I needed the money. Besides, I loved teaching and was fond of my pupils. All of this turned over in my head, but I was resolved to go on with my decision. Had I expected things to be easy? In all the books it was manifest that sacrifices had to be made.

When Mr. Owen arrived I made him a cup of coffee to propitiate him, and then took the plunge. I said I needed to give up my Thursday class.

"May I ask why?" he said.

Some instinct made me tell him the truth. I said I had found a way of studying a philosophy of life that would enable me to become a better person. Perhaps because he was so acutely aware of the need for me to become a better person, Mr. Owen changed his manner completely. This brusque peppery man became mellow. He put his hand on my shoulder and said: "I'm sure that you are doing the right thing, and I hope you find happiness! Don't worry about the class, I will sort it out just leave all that to me."

The next moment he was gone, and I sank on to a chair in amazement. If a genie had suddenly appeared in the room I couldn't have been more surprised.

Dolores phoned me later. "Where were you?" she said. "I caught the train and you weren't on it!"

"What did you do?" I asked.

"I waited at Euston Station to see if you were in the back part of the train, but when I was sure you weren't on it I took the next train home."

"It turned out for the best," I said. "It was important for me to see Dr. A. alone. But you can make an appointment to see him alone too." Dolores made an evasive answer, and after that I never saw her again.

On the following Thursday Dr. A. welcomed me to the group for the first time. There I met Mrs. A., a beautiful white-haired woman with a figure as dainty as a piece of porcelain, which seemed too small to contain her powerful spirit.

The others in the group were trying to find a meaning to their lives, as I was. Some had been brought there by suffering, some had found their way there through a search of their own. Looking back, it seems to me that I joined the group in the nick of time. Without the support of the group and the help of our teachers, Dr. and Mrs. A., I would not have been able to bear the terrible things that were about to come upon me.

Chapter Twenty-five

Berkhamsted School

At Westbrook, Danny's school, it was the tradition for boys to board in their final year. Danny was thirteen that year and so well-adjusted that we thought we could risk it and let him board. Danny himself liked the idea because all the other boys were boarding, and it marked a step in his growing manhood.

Before he went I thought I ought to give him a little talk on the possible difficulties he might encounter of a sexual nature. I hemmed and hawed, talking about problems he might encounter at night in the dormitory. Danny watched me with a grin and said finally, "Mum, are you trying to tell me I mustn't let myself get buggered?"

I decided he was sophisticated enough to cope by himself.

He went off happily and we saw him on Sundays when he came to church with the other Catholic boys in the school, and on the holidays. During his Easter break, I arranged a special day out for him: he and I went to lunch at Dorothy England's house. She was a great cook and we had a delightful time with her.

After this we all three walked down to the convent nearby where Sister Seraphina, a nun who was a great friend of mine, gave us a beautifully laid out tea. Her cousin, Father Michael, was also there.

The atmosphere was very peaceful, as it often is in a convent. Danny relaxed, and for the first time he spontaneously spoke about his epilepsy. Father Michael listened sympathetically and then assured him that it was not a great disability. He told Danny of many people he had known who had been successful despite being epileptic.

Danny listened, and a hopeful smile began to spread over his face. On the way home he sighed contentedly and said, "That was the best day of my life."

Boarding at school helped Danny academically. When the exam results came out in the summer, we learned that Danny had come second in the whole county in Latin, and that he had been accepted into Berkhamsted School, a Public school that was hard to get into.

We went to see Berkhamsted School; the headmaster showed us round, and when I saw the basketball equipment I exclaimed, "Oh Danny, you should be good at that because you are so tall!" He answered dryly, "It does need a certain skill as well."

The school buildings and grounds looked lovely. I was elated that Danny had got into such a famous school. Everything was ready for him to go, when Jim suddenly telephoned me from his office. He had misgivings; he thought, after all, Danny should not go there. He asked me to telephone other schools to see if Danny could go somewhere else, but by this time it was too late, no school would take him at a moment's notice.

I was relieved. How could we have explained to Danny that we had changed our minds? Also, he was to go with other boys from his year at Westbrook. I told myself that by now they were all his friends, that boarding with them had made all the difference. Still, his father's fears for Danny troubled me, and I worried a lot. In the end it seemed easiest to take the chance and let Danny go.

At first it appeared that my husband's fears were without foundation. Danny appeared to have made the adjustment.

He used to walk to school along the canal. It was three miles, but he always loved walking and preferred it to taking the train or a taxi.

I watched with an anxious heart as he set out every morning, trudging down the hill and along the canal. He never complained, no matter what the weather conditions were like. Sometimes he would come home in the pouring rain, looking like a drowned rat.

I asked him many times about his time at school, but he didn't say much. As we didn't hear anything to the contrary from the school, we assumed everything was going well.

At Christmas, Danny's old school, Westbrook, gave an Old Boys Reunion dinner. The boys were invited to bring a girlfriend, and Danny invited me to go with him as his "bird." It was a pleasant evening and a lovely dinner with the headmaster and his wife presiding.

Danny sat with his age group at another table. From time to time I glanced over to see how he was doing, and felt my heart ache. Danny was isolated from the other boys; their jokes didn't include him. He was, as he had once said, "a lonely chap." I hoped that things were different at Berkhamsted School. Perhaps he had made friends there.

On Danny's fourteenth birthday, Dorothy England came over again to make it a party.

In the summer we were all invited by my parents for a holiday in America. Jim did not want to go, he seemed unhappy and anxious to get away by himself, so in the end he went to a chateau in France where he was taught French as part of the holiday. I took the boys over to visit my parents in Maine. They had rented a house by the shore, and enrolled the boys in a sailing course. The house also had a sailing dinghy in the boathouse which the boys would be allowed to use.

Danny and Tommy proved to be complete landlubbers, but Charles loved sailing right away and explained to us all how the laws of wind and gravity determined the direction of the boat.

After his first lesson in sailing, Charles went back to the house and pulled out the dinghy, my Mother and I clucking around him nervously like a pair of old hens. We stood on the edge of the water as Charlie sailed away, and from then on our view of Charlie was mostly a rust-coloured sail spotted from time to time on the horizon. My mother smiled at me one day as we looked at the little sail. "You can feel the waves of happiness coming from Charlie even here!" she said.

When my father came up for weekends he was very taken with the boys. Charles took him sailing and Tommy played tennis with him. Tommy took to tennis, and when my father left and he couldn't get anyone else to play with him he would coax Danny into playing.

My mother watched from the window and told me about it. "It was so sweet to see them together," she said. "Thomas was showing Danny how to play and cheering him on whenever he did well, and Danny was so humble, accepting all this from a younger brother."

Danny behaved well up to the very last day, when he quarrelled with his brothers over a television program. When they wouldn't let him watch the program he wanted, he hurled a chair through the window, smashing it and scattering glass everywhere. My father was very annoyed, but managed to get the window repaired before we left. Danny was made to apologise and was very glum for a while.

In spite of this my father had become very fond of the boys, and Mother told me that they were thinking of retiring and coming to live near us. They wanted to get to know all their grandchildren. I was delighted at the idea.

When we arrived back home, we greeted Jim, back from his holidays, and exchanged holiday stories. On Sunday Sheila and Shane and their girls came for lunch. When he heard that my parents were coming over here to live, Shane burst out laughing. Later he confided to me that Jim had told him when he first came to London that he was bringing me to England to get me away from my family!

Shortly afterwards my parents came to live in England and bought a house near us all. Mother decided to paint Danny's portrait, as she was interested in helping him. Danny loved going there and sitting for the picture. He became fond of my mother and was delighted with the portrait, which hung in my parents' dining room. When we went there for visits I would catch him standing in front of it, gazing at it with a pleased grin on his face.

Then it was time to get the boys ready for school. Danny was to go into his second year at Berkhamsted School. He did not seem very enthusiastic, but then neither did he complain.

Chapter Twenty-six

Breakdown

During the next term at Berkhamsted School Danny seemed to be getting more and more depressed. His fits started up again and he had to have stronger medication. This made him "dopey" and it was harder for him to concentrate on lessons at school. It seemed like a vicious circle—with the new drugs he found it harder to study, which brought on greater stress, and stress brought on more fits, leading to greater medication.

Jim and I both felt very unhappy about Danny's situation, but we kept hoping that he would settle down and adjust to the new pills. As we didn't hear anything from the school, we assumed that Danny was managing somehow, but it was heartbreaking to see him coming home so tired. He seemed to keep going with a kind of dogged endurance.

Then one day we were asked to come to the school and were given an appointment with the headmaster. When Danny heard that we were going to see the headmaster, he changed, and began to behave oddly. One day he came home with deep bloody scratches down his left arm as though he had been clawed by a wild animal.

"What happened to you?" I asked him, horrified.

"I did it with my compass," he said.

"But why?"

"To get the old skin off."

A feeling of horror and nausea came over me. As soon as I could I telephoned Miss Sandy to get her advice. She drove over right away and asked me to leave Danny alone with her as she wanted to do some tests with him. When she had finished, I asked her anxiously if she had discovered anything. Was there anything wrong? Could we do anything to help? She didn't answer me directly. She said, "There is something you can do."

"What?" I asked, ready to sacrifice anything for Danny.

She said a strange thing: "I want you to write down everything that Danny says."

I took this as an important task, thinking that maybe Miss Sandy needed this as a record so that she could understand Danny more. But as the days went by and I wrote Danny's words down, I was forced to look at what he was saying. And I began to see the thing I had been dodging for so long Danny's words no longer made sense. There was no logic to them; I might have been writing down the words of a madman. Still, I did not want to believe what I had been writing down. Danny could not be insane. This must be a passing phase.

Now the appointment came up and Jim and I went to see the headmaster of Berkhamsted School. Danny's house master was there as well. They both said that Danny's work was not good enough. He was not keeping up with the other boys. They felt perhaps the work was too difficult and he should leave.

We explained about the heavy medication Danny was on to stop his increasing fits. As soon as the fits settled the drugs could perhaps be reduced. But the headmaster's face remained unrelenting. He said that Danny had begun to behave strangely and it was disturbing the other boys.

Jim defended his son, saying that often the drugs had strange side effects, but I couldn't speak. I thought of all the things that Danny had said that I had written down, and I was filled with a terrible foreboding.

Meanwhile Jim persuaded the headmaster to give Danny another chance. He promised that he himself would supervise Danny's homework and would guarantee that it would be better done from now on. After that, every evening when Jim came home from work he went and sat in Danny's room while he did his homework. I felt very strongly that this was not the solution; it was just more pressure on Danny, who was no longer normal. The scraping of his arm haunted me, and I began to feel that it would be better after all if he did leave the school.

Another few days and the choice was out of our hands. A letter arrived from the school saying that Danny must leave by next term.

We discussed it together when the boys were in bed. Jim said that obviously the school didn't want the trouble of looking after Danny. "He's our problem." he said.

The next morning Jim went up to wake Danny as he was late for school. He hurried down looking grim. "He's taken an overdose of his pills," he said. I raced upstairs; Danny was lying in bed, his face a deathly grey-green.

As I looked at him I saw in that instant the image of Danny that we had so carefully built up over the years collapsing like a house of cards.

"Which pills did you take?" I asked urgently.

Danny pointed to the bottle of Tegretol, which I stored on his top shelf ready for putting in his envelopes. He had taken three quarters of it. I raced downstairs and telephoned the hospital. They told us to bring him into casualty.

When we brought him in, the nurses took him away. Jim had to go to work and I sat on a bench till a nurse called me and said I could see my son now. The doctors had pumped out his stomach, but as he had taken the overdose the night before, a lot of it had gone into his system and he would need several days under observation while he recovered.

I followed the nurse into the ward where Danny was lying in a hospital bed. I sat by him, and he glared at me in silence. At last I asked, "Why did you do it, Danny?"

A tragic look came over his face. "I'll never get a job," he said. "I'll never be able to earn my own living." For him the house of cards had collapsed, too.

"You both said, 'He's our problem,'" he added accusingly. "I listened behind the door and I heard you."

A few days later the hospital telephoned to say that Danny was fine and could be collected, but the doctor wanted to see me first.

The young doctor eyed me with hostility. He made it clear that he was critical of us as parents. He told me that my son's attempt on his life was remarkable in that he was so young, only fourteen. Was there anything wrong at home?

I was by now aware that we could have spared Danny suffering if we had acted earlier, that this school had been the wrong one, that Danny had been suffering far more than we had guessed. All of this welled up in me. I tried to answer but only burst into tears. The doctor watched me silently and then sent me to get Danny, who was still hostile and angry.

In the taxi going home Danny noticed my tears and said, "Why are you crying? It can't be for me, it must be for something else."

The hospital had made an appointment for Danny to go to a psychiatric clinic. They were to assess his situation and see where he could go to school. I thought perhaps he could go to the Rudolph Steiner school nearby, and we got an appointment to be interviewed.

I liked the school which was warm, pleasant and relaxed. But the woman there said that before Danny could be accepted he would have to be assessed by their psychiatrist in London. We went for the interview; an elderly man came and led Danny into a room where they remained for an hour. When they came out, the man said he would be writing to me. He avoided my eye.

A few days later a letter came, saying that they could not accept Danny at the school.

Danny continued to be depressed. He began to deteriorate rapidly in appearance. Since he had come home from the hospital he had refused to take a bath, or wash at all. He began to walk with his shoulders hunched; his hair grew long and greasy, but he would not let it be cut. After a few weeks he refused to join the family at meals; instead he would raid the larder late at night.

Next he took to wearing a towel over his head, complaining of the light. He would spend a day kneeling in front of a chair, his head on the cushions, covered in a towel and rocking gently. I tried to keep him company by sitting with him in the room and painting. I did my utmost to get him to talk, thinking if only I could reach him I might be able to help.I asked him what he would like if he could have anything he wanted. He said what he would like most of all would be to live deep underground where no one could get at him.

"But what would you do for food?" I asked.

He said, "It could be sent down in a lift."

All my efforts to reach him failed.

Danny smoked cigarettes, secretly at first, then more and more openly. One day I asked him if I could try a cigarette, too. When Danny saw me spluttering over the cigarette, a wintry smile crossed his face. He showed me how to smoke properly. However as his father was so against smoking I couldn't join Danny in the habit.

Jim tried hard to stop Danny smoking, but it was no use. They had terrible shouting matches but there was nothing Jim could do. There was no punishment that anyone could inflict on Danny greater than the punishments he was inflicting on himself.

After one shouting match between them Danny yelled at his father, "You are just an ignorant Irish peasant!" and turning to me he said, "You are getting old and ugly." As he stomped out, Jim said, "Tis your own know where to put the sword!" I realised Jim was right—Danny had an uncanny knack for knowing the places where we felt vulnerable.

As Danny's deterioration continued he began to hate us, his parents. One day he was sitting at the kitchen table with the radio on full blast.

"It's too loud," I said, reaching over to turn it down.

"Leave that alone! Get back!" shouted Danny.

Startled, I looked up at him. He had the face of a madman. He had grabbed the bread knife and was pointing it at me.

"Get back, or I'll kill you!" he shouted.

It was as if my child had been replaced by a demon. I felt a sickening lurch in my stomach. Then I heard myself talking to Danny in a high, gentle voice, "It's all right, Danny, I won't hurt you, don't be afraid."

Danny put down the knife and his face went back to being his own, though it was very gloomy. I tiptoed away to the hall where I saw eleven-year-old Tommy standing transfixed. "You were marvellous, Mum!" he said.

I smiled, trying to hide from him the fact that I had been so frightened.

Chapter Twenty-seven

Getting Danny Certified

Miss Sandy telephoned to see how we were and I begged her to come over, saying I needed her advice. I invited her for lunch. During the meal Danny sat in a corner with a towel over his face. Afterwards I asked her what to do about him. She said firmly that Danny ought not to be at home all the time. "It is affecting the other boys," she warned me. She left, promising to visit me again soon.

The next day I took Danny to the psychiatric clinic. The young woman there was new. She questioned me closely about Danny's history. I told her how difficult he had become.

"How do you get him to take his pills, then?" she asked.

I smiled. "Well, luckily we have a system of envelopes, so he doesn't think about it as an act of possible rebellion." I told her about the envelope system my mother had invented. She looked astonished. "And you kept it up, all this time?"

"Yes," I said, wondering at her surprise. Anything we could do for Danny helped ease our pain. It was the things we couldn't do that were hard to bear.

"Danny's problem," she told me, "is that he is unable to feel emotion. He is unable to love anyone."

"But that's not true!" I protested. "He does love people!"

"You have no proof of that," she said.

"No proof!" I tried desperately to recall events in the past pictures of Danny being so shattered when he saw me nursing baby Charles, then as a small child clinging to Charles when he came back from hospital; the times when Danny had called me his "bird"; his devotion to his father ...

"The Teasmade!" I exclaimed. "Danny saved up for a year to buy a Teasmade for his father."

I wanted to go on with other stories of Danny's helpless love for us, but I felt caught up again in the old web. She wasn't listening, she had already made up her mind about him. "You will have to take Danny to the doctor," she said. "It needs a doctor's certificate to certify a patient."

"*Certify!*" I recoiled from the word. How could I ask for Danny to be certified? It would be the end of all our efforts for so many years.

I talked it over with Jim that night. We tried to think of anything that might distract Danny from his terrible downward spiral. Jim thought up the idea of sending Danny on a train trip by himself. There was a cheap "Merrymaker" outing that he could go on which would take him to Manchester and back in a day. This seemed a good way of occupying Danny during the day, and giving him the feeling of independence.

But Danny had his own ideas. He went to Manchester, waited until the last train home had gone, and then telephoned his father to say he had missed it so that Jim had to drive all the way up north to collect him.

I thought of taking Danny for walks and treating him to lunch out somewhere. I found that if I could coax Danny out of the house and get him to go for a walk somewhere, the day would not be so bad. We did not exactly walk together; Danny would stride off in front as fast as he could while I struggled to keep up with him, or he would trail far behind, waiting until I was sufficiently far ahead. Still, he always seemed a little better when we had been out, though it was not always possible to persuade him to go.

On some days he was uncontrollable. We never knew what he was going to do next. One afternoon Charles and I watched Danny take all the eggs out of the fridge and slowly smash them on the floor. Neither of us tried to stop him because that made him violent and dangerous. There was a physical fear as he was now very big and strong, but there was also the fear of triggering off the appearance of the "madman" in Danny.

Afterwards Charlie confided to me that the thing he found hardest to take was Danny's illogicality. Charlie began to stay late at school, working on the school computer, and Tommy took refuge on the football field. I was thankful that they could get away sometimes, as Danny was now making life a misery for us all. He would put the radio on full blast at night, and shout and yell with the pop tunes. Jim got up several times in the night to try to stop him, but to no avail.

I worried about Jim. He had been so strong in the past, as strong as an oak tree while I had bent like a reed under the weight of our problems, but now I saw that in bending to the storm a reed could survive, while the defiant oak was in danger of being broken by the storm.

I realised that for the sake of all of us I would have to take Danny to the doctor and get him certified. Every day his behaviour became worse. He had started eating newspapers all day and spitting them out in little balls all over the house. He walked around with his trousers hanging down to his knees, which astonished any visitors still coming to the house.

But when I brought Danny to our trusted Dr. Sutton, he was kind but stubborn. He gazed at me and asked reproachfully, "Do you mean to say that you want me to certify him?"

I couldn't bring myself to say the words. I tried again to explain how difficult life was with Danny as he was now. Dr. Sutton examined Danny for a long time, then Danny came out and I went in. Dr. Sutton stuck to his original declaration he said that Danny was not schizophrenic, and there was nothing wrong with him.

I listened to what he was saying, my eyes fixed on the circle of newspaper spit balls that Danny had left on the surgery carpet.

What it amounted to was that we had to go on coping with Danny at home. It was getting harder and harder. Soon there was no area in which he was remotely normal.

When I saw him continually fingering the bread knife, fear overcame me and I took Danny back to the surgery and begged Dr. Sutton for help. But Dr. Sutton didn't want to hear what I was saying. It appeared that Danny would be certified and removed only if he did something really dreadful. I was in the hateful position of hoping that he would do something dreadful soon. Life had become unbearable for all of us.

We hadn't long to wait. Danny turned into a pyromaniac one day and started lighting fires everywhere. At last I was able to convince the doctor that he was dangerous. However, he was still unwilling to certify Danny.

He told us that he was sending Danny to Bart's Hospital in London for two weeks to have his drugs looked at. After that he would see what was to be done.

Chapter Twenty-eight

Bethlem

It was an incredible relief to get rid of Danny, even though we knew it was just for two weeks. I went to visit him in Bart's Hospital. There was the ward, all the patients tucked neatly into the spotless white beds in rows. Under one empty bed two large feet stuck out on the floor Danny was lying under the bed. He wouldn't come out and greet me, so what conversation we had was conducted by me peering under the bed.

The next visit was even more unpropitious. This time Danny was sitting among all the wheelchairs stacked in the dark hallway. He had chosen the one furthest away, in a corner. When he saw me he got into a furious rage.

"Why did you come here!" he shouted. "I'd like to kick you in the stomach!"

Later, after Gran went to visit Danny, she came to see us and said she'd spoken to a pretty young nurse who had told her that "all Danny needs is a little love." Gran gave a derisive snort, "I wonder how she would have coped with him these last months!"

Back at home after a few days without Danny we all began to unwind. That's when I realised fully what a strain we'd all been under. I knew I couldn't go back to looking after Danny at home. I telephoned Miss Sandy in desperation and asked her what I could do. She was very supportive, and more important, she understood how the system worked.

"Here is what you must do," she said. "You must ask to see the hospital psychiatrist. Tell him that you are worried. Say that Danny attacked you with a knife and tell him that the younger children are afraid of him. It is important to put your case well. You must forget about being brave now. It is essential to convince them that something must be done at once. Make a scene if necessary."

I made an appointment and went to the hospital to see the psychiatrist. I went in nervously, knowing everything depended on this interview. All my upbringing and social training so far had gone into keeping a stiff upper lip, being brave and not complaining. Now I had to go against all that and make a scene. I felt all the pent-up grief inside me in a hard knot, but I couldn't get it out.

The psychiatrist was a woman, so I felt a little better. I sat down and told her about Danny. She listened in silence, then asked about his childhood. I told her about the early days when we'd been told he was schizophrenic, and then found that he was epileptic.

"Was he very badly epileptic?" she asked.

"At one stage he was having fits every quarter of an hour," I told her.

She looked at me in sympathy. "That must have been very hard on you." Her compassion seemed to release the hard knot inside me.

"Yes," I said, "it was hard but I was able to manage, and I was glad to manage, I could cope with everything until now, but I just can't cope anymore!" The flood of tears came now and I didn't try to hold them back. Between sobs I told her of the terrible time we'd had and how I was afraid for my children and myself when my husband wasn't there. Her face was filled with compassion and she promised that she would do her best to help me.

Just before Danny was due to return home from Bart's Hospital, we were informed that he was to be transferred to the Maudsley Hospital, where Jim and I were to go to be interviewed. There an intelligent, rather brisk doctor interviewed us, asking if there were any problems in our marriage. By tacit agreement we were reticent about our personal differences, but open about everything else.

One thing the doctor was emphatic about: he wanted to be very sure that Danny had never been involved in taking drugs, other than the ones he needed to control his fits. We were able to reassure him on that score. His own drugs were abhorrent enough for Danny.

Then the doctor told us that he proposed to send Danny to the Royal Bethlem Hospital in Croydon, where there was an adolescent unit for sixteen boys and sixteen girls.

There was a waiting list of three years, but they had decided to take Danny right away as they felt they might be able to help him. We, his parents, would have to co-operate in the treatment, however, and this meant that at first we had to promise not to try to contact Danny in any way for six weeks.

"Six weeks!" we exclaimed. It sounded like heaven.

"Yes, I know it's a long time," the doctor said sympathetically, "but you must trust us."

"We do!" we said fervently. "Take even longer if you need to."

The doctor told us that we could collect Danny in the other room and take him straight down to Bethlem hospital. We went to locate him and found that he had locked himself in the toilet and was busy strewing the place with toilet paper. With a lot of cajoling and threatening we managed to get him out and into the car.

It was a long drive down to the Bethlem. At last we came to some huge iron gates and drove through to a large stone building. We went up some stone steps to a recreation room where everything was nailed down or fixed to the wall. There were iron bars on all the windows.

We were led to a small, spartan room containing a single iron bed. Danny looked at the room and a slow smile spread over his face. I realised then what he must have suffered being in a huge ward of people when he so much wanted to be alone. We set down his suitcase and said goodbye with relief.

As we were leaving I turned back on impulse and said, "Danny, the hospital doctor said that you are not insane. They say that they can help you to get better here. We are not allowed to see you for six weeks, but we can see you after that and try and help you get better again."

He didn't answer but his eyes met mine, and I felt that he had listened to what I was saying.

As we drove out of the iron gates we felt dizzy with relief. Jim said with sardonic humour, "Right now, quick! Off to South America!"

Chapter Twenty-nine

Visits

Six weeks later we were asked to come and pay Danny a visit. We drove down to Bethlem taking the two younger boys with us. Danny seemed quite pleased to see us; that is to say, he didn't hurl abuse at us, but silently showed us round the place.

Charles and Tommy just stared at the metal bars on the windows and were glad to get away.

Neill, the male nurse at Bethlem, asked to speak with Jim and me. He told us that we would be part of a team working to help Danny. The idea was that visits home and visits from us to Bethlem were to be regarded as rewards for good behaviour. If Danny behaved badly, the visits were to be withdrawn. In this way Danny could be induced to become more co-operative.

Neill and the other staff members seemed to understand quite a lot about Danny. Neill told us that he was regarded as somewhat of a character. On his first evening there, he refused to go into the communal room but sat all evening in the staff room reading one of their books, entitled *The Four-year-old in an Urban Environment.*

Neill pointed to a list on the wall. It read: Words Daniel Is Not Allowed to Use:

Dunno	No
Won't	Maybe
Perhaps	

Neill said, "We had to do this because Danny was so taciturn that he was using these words instead of conversing." He added that Danny had already begun to alter his ways a little. He had a sense of humour and could even appreciate a joke against himself.

We learned that one of most important parts of the treatment was the Monday morning get-together. All the doctors and psychiatrists were there, together with the staff and patients. At this meeting everything was discussed, grievances were aired and everyone had a say. This helped people to see and understand different points of view.

I was impressed by Neill's no-nonsense approach to the situation. For the first time the thought struck me that maybe we had been too indulgent to Danny. We had been so aware of his problems that we had tended to let him have what he wanted whenever we could. Maybe this had not been helpful to him in the long run.

A few days later Neill phoned us to say that Danny was due to make his first visit home. He was to be fetched on the next weekend. I felt sick with dread. I couldn't overcome my past fears.

At Dr. A.'s Thursday evening group, which I continued to attend, I told him about my fears and asked him for help. He sat silently for a while, then he said, "Believe me, I know that fear well. Don't try to do anything from yourself. Instead, when you can, sit quietly and ask for help from something higher."

I remembered the time when Danny had first threatened me and I had been able to speak to him in a way that would calm him. It was as if I had been given the right words to say then. Perhaps I just had to go on trusting that I would be given the help I needed.

The first visit home from Danny went very well and I knew I would not be so nervous the next time.

On the following weekend Danny had to be visited at Bethlem and taken out for the day. I set out early in the morning because it was a long journey train, underground, train and bus. When I went to fetch Danny he was standing by a huge dark bush, with his head bent. It was such a sad sight on this lovely sunny day, to see this fine strong boy just standing there, hiding, with his head down.

Why? I thought once again, why does it have to be like this for him? Why can none of us help?

"Hello, Danny!" I said, hating myself for the forced jolliness in my voice, "I've come to take you out!"

No response, but at least no hostility. I smiled at him and received a flicker of recognition.

"Can you show me any restaurants around here? We could go and have lunch together," I proposed, still walking on eggshells.

Silently, Danny came out from behind his bush and started striding down the avenue to the gate. I followed him, running as usual to keep up with his long strides. When we reached the town we saw a Chinese restaurant. "Shall we try this?" I asked. Without a word, Danny brushed past me. We ate our way through Set Meal B for Two Persons, including Chinese tea, in total silence.

Afterwards we went to a book shop where I bought Danny a magazine. He chose one that had horoscopes in it. With great excitement he pointed out his horoscope of the day, which said, "You will lead a dazzling social life!" Danny spoke at last: "Look, Mum, you see," he cried, "that was our Chinese lunch!"

After this the pattern was established; every second weekend Jim would collect Danny and drive him home, and on the alternate weekends I would go to Bethlem to take Danny out for the day.

It was always an effort to go through the great iron gates. Despite the beautiful exterior of the building and the spacious grounds, Bethlem Hospital was a gloomy place. Everything that could be done to improve the atmosphere had been done, but the misery of the patients there seemed to cling to the walls and furniture in an almost palpable smoky layer.

I always had to force myself to enter that building and I never left the gates without a huge feeling of relief. I would walk down to the bus stop taking great gulps of clean air, as though I were washing my lungs of all the depression that I had breathed in while I was inside.

Chapter Thirty

Magic

During all this time the group on Thursdays had been my chief support. I was now invited to join an extra class on Friday evenings which was doing sacred movements. These movements called for the best attention one could bring. We were given first a rhythm for the feet, then a different rhythm for the arms and a third movement for the head. I found that it was impossible to do these movements by straining, or trying to do them with the mind. The only way was to let go and allow the body to do them.

In this way it was possible to feel and understand that the body has a special power of its own, not just a physical power but a spiritual one as well. Through this way my body gradually became a great help and anchor to me. Then I realised how ignorant I had been when I had wanted to soar into the air and leave my body behind!

When sitting in meditation every day I saw that it was possible to relax the tensions in my body, and gradually something began to ease inside me. But as the day progressed ordinary life took over and I could see how tense I usually was. All my past difficulties with Danny, waiting for him to have a fit, or trying to stop him being destructive, had made me nervous and tense. It was as if I was tensing up, waiting for the next bad thing to happen.

I asked Dr. A. about this and he said, "You know, events in life are like a chess board. There are the good times and bad times just as there are the black and white squares on the chess board. But we have the power to shrink the black squares and broaden the white ones."

"How?" I asked.

He gave me a wry smile. "Haven't you noticed how dread of a dental appointment can spoil a whole week?" I nodded.

"Well, the secret is to try to live in the moment. Do what is necessary in the present moment and let go of the future. Your younger boys need you to bring some happiness into their lives now."

I thought over what he had said and then I made a bargain with myself. I would do all that was necessary and right for Danny, and then for the other part of my life I would shut the door on him and his problems and try to make as happy a life as possible for the family and myself.

Next time Charles brought home a friend, I invited him to a formal dinner. Charlie was startled. "You're treating him like a grown-up!" he said.

"Well, you're fourteen now," I reminded him. "It won't be long before you are grown-up." Then I thanked him, saying I'd noticed that he was being very thoughtful and considerate at an age when most boys usually start to rebel.

Charlie gave me a shy smile. "You went through so much with Danny," he said. "I decided I wanted to be as little trouble as possible."

However, Charles and Tommy did enjoy teasing me. As the old saying goes, A mother's place is in the wrong! I was fond of using analogies when I gave advice to the boys, but one day my children turned the tables on me.

Charlie said to his brother, "Thomas, you must play your best in the great Football Field of Life!" And Tommy responded, "Ah, but Charles, remember that you are but a Test-tube in the Laboratory of Time!"

"Aw, shush!" I said.

"Now, Mum, this is but a Brushstroke on the Canvas of ..."

I chased them out of the kitchen.

On one Thursday, Dr. A. asked to see my painting. I brought in a book of my paintings and explained my beloved Mische technique that I had learned from Ernst Fuchs. Dr. A. looked at the elaborate paintings and said, "Will you do something for me?"

"Of course," I said immediately.

"Then I'd like you to do a water-colour for me."

I was startled. "But I only do the Mische technique!" I said proudly. His eyes gleamed at me behind his spectacles. "Yes, that's why I want you to do a water-colour."

I went home and thought it over. At last, grumbling to myself, I dug out my old box of water-colours and started a painting. It was very difficult to let go of my carefully acquired skills, and in trying to work spontaneously I produced a series of failures. Then one evening I saw a crow standing very velvety black on the shining green lawn and I rushed to capture the freshness of this impression.

It was as if I were looking with new eyes and opening another door in myself. I remembered what Dr. A. had told me how we inhabit a great mansion but only live in one room. Thanks to him, I had just moved into a new room!

When I brought him the water-colour I thanked him. "It was just like magic!" I said.

He nodded. "You will find that there is magic in this system. Real magic!"

I soon felt the need for all the help I could get, for just when my life had settled down on an even keel, on my next visit to Bethlem I was informed that Danny would be coming home for two weeks at Christmas. I battled with the old fear again, but was determined not to give in. We would cope. The important thing was to get Danny a Christmas present that he wanted. Then there would be a good chance of everything running smoothly.

However, Danny didn't seem to wish for anything. Then two weeks before Christmas, Danny told us that there was something he really wanted: a game called "Take the Brain." One of the boys in the ward had got it, and Danny had enjoyed playing it. He said it was the only thing he wanted. Overjoyed to think we could buy him something that would make him happy, I rushed out to the shops, only to be told that it was last year's game and they didn't stock it anymore. I went from Halstead to London, but it was unobtainable.

Two days before Christmas I was desperate. Then a friend offered to drive me to Watford to find this game; there was a big department store called Clements, which would be my last chance.

As I approached the counter, I became aware of a strange voice inside me saying, "Don't just ask for the game, make a story of it. Tell her your son is sick and in hospital and this is all he wants for Christmas."

"She won't be interested," I responded to myself. "I will only make a fool of myself. Either she has the game or not, what difference will it make whether I tell her about my son?"

Nevertheless, I decided to follow the "voice" and told the saleslady about my sick son in hospital who only wanted this "Take the Brain" game for Christmas. The saleslady was indeed unmoved. She said, "That was last year's game!" and turned away.

"There!" I told myself, "I needn't have bothered."

Suddenly a man spoke behind me, making me jump. He had been standing there so silently I hadn't noticed him.

"We have the game at home," he said. "You can have it if you like, for your boy."

His name was Mr. Talbot, and next day he came out with his family for a visit to bring us the game. We were able to give him some games for his son, ones that Danny was tired of. The son was very pleased. He was a year older than Danny, and he was schizophrenic.

We asked Mr. Talbot what he did for a living and he told us that he was a magician!

That Christmas was the Christmas of the "Take the Brain" game. Danny was the champion player, he was rarely beaten. The rest of the family spent our time taking turns at being beaten by him. His success at this game did a lot for his self-confidence, and it forced him to relate to people again as he couldn't play the game by himself.

Danny behaved comparatively well over the holiday. It appeared that the policy of the Bethlem hospital, that of making visits home a reward and withdrawal of these a punishment, was beginning to have an effect. Danny appeared to value my visits to him and to appreciate coming home more and more, especially when Sheila and Shane and their girls came to lunch.

He enjoyed especially playing "Take the Brain" with Roisin, Sheila's eldest girl, who was growing very pretty. Through the game they established a real friendship, and when Danny heard that Roisin was starting to collect stamps, he went up to his room and came down with his treasured stamp albums, a collection he had built up over many years. He placed them all in Roisin's hands. "They are for you." he said.

Roisin stared at him, amazed that he was giving them to her.

Danny beamed, and added shyly: "They might be worth some money one day." After that he hurried upstairs and hid in his room.

Chapter Thirty-one

Making Connections

After this improvement Danny regressed again. The Bethlem Hospital telephoned us to say that Danny's next weekend home had been cancelled as he had been behaving badly. When I went to take Danny out the following weekend, Neill had a word with me about him.

"The trouble is that Danny's made friends with a real nutter in here," Neill told me, "and he's started imitating him. We had to put him in a strait jacket in the padded cell."

I shuddered. Neill smiled reassuringly. "He's all right now. I think he frightened himself!"

Danny was obliging and docile on that visit!

Spring passed and with it Danny's sixteenth birthday. Mary Hill, a friend from my art school in Dublin, had married and lived near Bethlem Hospital. When they heard about Danny they were incredibly kind. They had a car and drove Danny and me to museums and restaurants. Danny enjoyed these outings so much his behaviour became almost normal.

One day we drove to a beautiful view. Danny asked if we could stop the car, and he got out and gazed at it for a long time.

"It's lovely, isn't it?" he said. His eyes were full of tears.

I nodded, I couldn't speak. It was the first time I had seen him lifted out of himself for years. When I returned home, I telephoned Miss Sandy to tell her about it.

"Well, you know he is your son," she replied. "He's bound to be sensitive to beauty."

On the next weekend that Danny was home, he sat in front of my latest painting for a long time. "What does it mean?" he asked me.

"What do you think it means?" I answered. I was flattered that he was interested in the painting and wanted to know what he was thinking.

To my amazement he responded with a detailed analysis of the picture. He interpreted all the symbolism correctly, saying that the creatures in the foreground represented difficulties and despair, but the sun rising in the background was more important. "That represents hope!" he said.

He gave me one of his rare and lovely smiles and I dared to hope that his depression might be lifting.

But with Danny a step forward was often followed by a step back. Two weeks later on a visit home, Danny behaved very badly. He ripped up the album I had made of him when he was a baby, tearing all the photos of himself in half.

When his father went upstairs and saw what Danny had done he was angry. Danny came down and yelled at us, then went up again and slammed his door. We decided that he should be sent back early to Bethlem as a punishment, and told him so. Danny came down looking repentant. "I'm sorry I was rude," he said.

We were flabbergasted. Danny had never apologised for anything in his life before! "That's all right," we said.

"What about the album you tore?" asked his father.

Danny made a nervous, brushing-away gesture with his hand. "I was sick," he said simply.

I began to understand what the Monday get-togethers in Bethlem were all about. It was clear that they made a distinction between those things which you could help and those you couldn't.

On the next weekend that Danny was due home, he arrived with a black eye. "How did you get that?" I asked.

"One of the boys hit me," he said.

"That's awful!" I began, but Danny stopped me.

"No, it wasn't his fault. He thought I was trying to steal his bike. I was just moving it so I could watch the television, but he thought I was going to take it and that's why he hit me."

This was a new thing coming from Danny. Always in the past if people attacked him he wanted instant revenge. He had never been interested in their motives before. He was beginning to make connections. I thought that he, too, was struggling to understand himself.

My respect for the Bethlem methods increased more and more.

Danny was obviously thinking over his problems and how to deal with them. One weekend after he had gone back, I found a scrap of paper in his room. On one side he had drawn a downward spiral with the words:

boredom
  apathy
    depression
      violence

I wondered if this were part of the method at Bethlem to see the mechanisms of mental illness.

On the other side of the scrap of paper Danny had written a description of himself: "Tall, thin, sad. Nervous, demure, wracked by epileptic fits. Lucky." This last word probably referred to his wins at bingo in Kuwait, but it had been so heavily crossed out it was hard to read.

Danny's fits increased in number and changed dramatically in character. Instead of falling to the ground in convulsions as before, he would hurtle forward as if shot from a cannon! He always seemed to pick extremely dangerous places to have these fits, so it took all our vigilance to prevent him having a messy and violent death while he was home for the weekends. On one weekend he arrived covered in bandages and my husband could not drive him back, so I had to take him on the most nerve-wracking trip of my life. Every place we went through was fraught with danger. Danny seemed to be able to bring on a fit in the worst places. I stood near, ready to grab him in an instant.

At the top of the stone steps at Euston station he shot by me and I grabbed his anorak just in time. There was more danger on the high escalator in the underground, but it wasn't so bad because the crowd prevented any major damage. We boarded the train for Croydon, and as we got off it at Croydon I breathed a sigh of relief only to see Danny hurtle past me towards the now moving train. Again I grabbed his anorak is it flew past, and Danny's head missed the train by inches. Then he lay on the ground in a coma.

The stationmaster came hurrying up in great excitement and a huge crowd began to collect in a circle around Danny, twittering anxiously.

Suddenly Danny opened his eyes, glared up at the crowd, and said loudly and clearly, "Why don't you all fuck off?"

The station cleared as if by magic, and the stationmaster and I were left looking at each other. "I don't blame him!" he said, and helped Danny to his feet.

We completed the last lap of the journey without fits.

I asked Jennifer, my friend who was epileptic, how much control Danny had over his fits, as I felt he had deliberately picked the most dangerous places to have them. She pondered for a bit and then said, "It's like crying. Sometimes you feel like crying but you can stop it, or you can let yourself cry; at other times you have to cry, you can't help it."

When I next went to Bethlem to take Danny out, I spoke to Neill and told him how nervous I was, taking Danny out as he was now.

Neill told me that they had achieved very good results by punishing Danny for having fits. They found that he could control them much more than he let on. "Tell him you won't take him out unless he promises not to have a fit," he advised.

I did this and Danny duly promised not to have a fit if I would take him to the Whitgift Shopping Centre. He loved huge shopping malls.

The Centre was crowded with people as it was Christmas time; I had to run to keep up with Danny's long strides. I was still afraid that he would have one of those dreadful fits. At last we stopped at a self-service restaurant and I sent Danny to find a table for two while I got us something to eat.

I was waiting in the queue when Danny came and touched my sleeve. "I'm sorry," he began, then he fell backwards in a fit, convulsing on the floor. This time he had not shot forward so it was not so dangerous. After he'd recovered, we sat and had our tea and he apologised again. I told him it was all right when he had fits like that one, and gave me warning. It was the other kind of fits I couldn't cope with.

After I brought him back to Bethlem I had a talk with Neill and told him what had happened. "The poor boy was apologising for having a fit!" I said. "I felt so mean."

Neill smiled. "I'm sure he couldn't help that one. Christmas shopping at the Whitgift Centre would give me a fit too!"

Chapter Thirty-two

The Thursday Group

One of the things Dr. A. had told me was, "Don't believe anything because I say it. Only believe what you experience yourself to be true."

As I continued the work of self-study, experiences began to happen. I saw useless habits and I tried to struggle with them, but for that it was necessary to "wake up." Gurdjieff said that the biggest obstacle to development is the fact that we are "asleep" most of the time. Of course, it is not easy to wake up; the Bible is full of reminders to keep awake, not to sleep but to watch and pray. But how is it possible to wake?

I began to learn that one thing that can help us is attention, the intentional direction of the mind. It is very difficult to sustain. Dr. A. told us we could not keep our attention on something for more than five minutes.

I couldn't believe this. I could paint for eight hours at a time. But maybe, I thought hopefully, my attention was more developed than the others? Looking at our disbelieving faces, Dr. A. gave us a task to see how long we could direct our attention. We were to look at an object any object and try to trace its origins, how it had come to be made, the causes of its being made, and so on.

Sitting alone at the breakfast table next morning I picked a jar of lime marmalade. It shone with a beautiful greeny-gold as the light filtered through it.

How had it come there? I had bought it at Sainsbury's, attracted by the colour. I thought of the people who had picked the fruit in a sunny land, the manufacturer who had set up a factory to process the fruit, the recipe for the marmalade which must have been older than all the machines, the glass itself which was first discovered as the nomads made fires in the desert and found the sand melted into glass. I looked again at the colour of the marmalade and a new thought occurred to me.

We never eat blue food! We eat food of all the other colours. Blueberries seem to be an exception but if you rub the bloom off the skin you can see they are purple, I had often done this in Canada ...

I "woke up" again several hours later. I had gone out shopping and was clearing the table. The sight of the marmalade jar reminded me. I had intended to stay with the jar for half an hour, but I had rushed away after only five minutes! It was as if a hand had come and wiped away my memory. I tried several times more, but I couldn't keep my attention on any object for more than five minutes.

I began to understand that nothing would develop in me unless I made a real effort. Yet the kind of effort I was used to making didn't help. It was no use pushing energy outward, or blaming myself for failure, as I was used to doing. The only kind of work that helped was a different kind of effort, a "letting go." Paradoxically, this was the hardest thing to do. In letting go I had to face what I was and accept my own emptiness. This was very hard to bear. Only a belief and trust in something on a higher level could help me at those moments.

In my studies about Gurdjieff's system, I had read that we have three centres: mind, emotions and body. But in most of us today, these centres are fragmented. The mind can think one thing, the emotions feel another thing, and the body can do a third thing. Not only that, but the different centres can interfere with each other. I hadn't quite grasped how one centre could interfere with another until I experienced it for myself.

One day I was walking down the High Street in Halstead, worrying about preparing for a journey with Danny. I had to get a large supply of pills, to collect the travel tickets and to withdraw money from the bank. All these things were spinning around in my head when I suddenly "woke up."

In a flash I saw my inner state. In my mind I was buying the tickets and collecting the pills in advance, I was doing this with great force, exhausting myself uselessly, while my feelings and anxieties about the journey had seeped into my body, so that my heart was thumping and my legs were trembling.

I was so interested by this discovery that I was able to stop, and when I tried to relax, the great tensions began to ease and I felt as if I had truly "pulled myself together."

Dr. A. often gave us exercises to try during the week. One week he suggested that we all try not to run for buses and trains. I was startled. I always ran for buses! How could I not? I might miss my bus otherwise, and then what would I do? Nevertheless I decided to try.

One day at the bus stop I was waiting with a huge crowd for a delayed bus. At last one came along, but it was doubtful if we would all fit on it. I began to elbow my way forward to make sure I had a place, when suddenly I remembered the exercise.

But this is not running for a bus, I argued. Then I saw it was worse than running—it was like a huge hypnotic force, driving us to fight our way on regardless of the others. I stopped for a moment and tried to look at the power of that force. It was like a huge magnet. What was so important about that bus? I decided to walk the three miles home, sickened by the strength of the force at the bus stop. I could see how people could easily be trampled to death once that force took control.

When I told Dr. A. about it, he said, "We are told that this is the force that keeps us all in slavery!"

He added with a twinkle in his eye, "A devil sits on your left shoulder and an angel sits on your right, and you need them both. Our place is in the struggle between them."

Everyone in the group spoke of his or her experiences, and I began to notice how I loved to show off when telling what I had found. The more I looked into myself, the more I encountered things I didn't like. Old fears came back, of the darkness inside, of the possible madness, of evil itself as an overwhelming force.

One evening Mrs. A. saw me shivering in the hallway, and drew me into the study to ask what was the matter.

"I'm so afraid!" I said.

"Why are you afraid?" I told her of my old fear of madness.

"But you are not mad!" she said, almost impatiently. I stared at her. Was it that simple? Perhaps it was. One of my old fears began to slide away. I groped around for another to bring out into the open.

"I'm afraid to look inside ... afraid of what I might see." Her hazel eyes gazed serenely into mine. "If it is true, what is there to fear?"

I was reassured by her matter-of-factness. If something was true, perhaps there was no reason to fear. I repeated these words to myself like a mantra. This gave me the courage to go on looking, and what I saw was not illimitable evil, but small meanesses and greeds.

I remembered G. K. Chesterton's fable about a man who spent his life running away from a monster. The more he fled, the bigger and more terrible the monster grew. Then one day he stopped fleeing and forced himself to turn and face the monster. It fled from him and he pursued it until it disappeared into a cave. He went into the cave and when he pulled the creature out into the light, it was only a smelly old goat.

I found that learning about my dark side had an interesting effect. I found that all that I had been taught in the convent school about "evil" had not been helpful; it was a kind of projecting outwards of anything I didn't accept about myself.

By accepting my shadow side I gained a new force. It became like manure that I could use to grow roses. With this energy I could find strength to endure the problems in my life.

The interesting thing about this self-study was that it didn't seem to lead to mere introspection; instead, I was becoming more aware of other people. My Catholic religion was still important to me, but I began to see that there was truth and depth in other religions as well, and that sometimes they could express a truth which had been forgotten in our own faith.

One day Dr. A. asked us to go for a walk and observe how we looked at things. I tried this one afternoon when I went on a visit to my friend Jennifer. All the gardens along the road going up to her house were beautifully tended, and there were blossoming trees everywhere.

Then I noticed something about the way I was looking at everything. There was something acquisitive about it. Whenever I saw something beautiful I wanted to paint it or photograph it, in order to somehow possess it.

On my next walk I tried to look at things without my usual acquisitiveness, to let go of my usual self and just be there. And a strange thing happened. I was looking at a lovely blossoming tree. It was a pink hawthorn and the colours were unusually rich and deep. Suddenly the blossom tree widened out to embrace the whole world, and I felt that I was no longer a single individual but a part of the vast universe. This feeling lasted only for a few seconds and then it vanished. However I never forgot that moment.

As time went by my relationship with people in the Thursday group began to deepen. It was such a relief to leave one's clamourous ordinary self outside the door and sit together in an inner room.

Then as each person spoke of his or her inner struggle, I began to feel that it was my struggle too. We came, all of us, to trust each other, and something like love grew between us all.

Sometimes we just sat in silence. A feeling of peace would descend in those moments and a deep joy that stayed with me for a long time, and seemed a reassurance that, after all, behind everything in the world there was hope.

Chapter Thirty-three

An Incident

Once when Danny was visiting Jennifer he said to her, "They put me in an insane asylum because I have strange thoughts." At the same time, he had become used to Bethlem and even attached to it, so it was a shock to him and to us when Bethlem Hospital contacted us and said that they thought Danny had been there long enough. They said he was in danger of becoming institutionalised. He had been there since he was fifteen, and now he was nearly eighteen. They wrote that he was not schizophrenic and that he should now leave.

It was a blow to us. Greatly as Danny had improved in the years that he had been there, he was still far from normal. We all felt nervous at the thought of having him home all the time.

We went to a meeting at the Bethlem to discuss Danny's future. We asked the doctors and psychiatrists where Danny could go if he had to leave Bethlem. They said that they would see if they could recommend somewhere, but they made it clear to us that it was not their responsibility.

Danny himself did not want to leave Bethlem. Keenly as he felt the stigma attached to being there, he had got used to the place and he was afraid of change.

On my next visit Neill told me that Danny was upset when the doctor told him he needn't stay there because he wasn't insane. Danny had insisted that he *was* insane! I was puzzled over the question, and asked Miss Sandy when next

I saw her, "If Danny isn't schizophrenic, as the doctors at Bethlem insist, then why does he behave so oddly?"

"Well, there are degrees," she said. "He could be schizoid, for example, or have schizoid tendencies."

I gave it up. It was too technical for me.

That weekend Danny came home for a visit in a bad mood. I had flu and was in bed with a temperature. Jim drove Danny and Charles into the town on a shopping expedition, but soon I was woken from a feverish sleep by the insistent ringing of the telephone. I flung myself out of bed to answer it.

It was the police. The sergeant said, "We have your son here. He was apprehended by a store detective stealing books and other commodities from Woolworth's. Can you come to the police station and collect him?"

I tried to organise my thoughts. This seemed like a feverish nightmare!

"I'm sorry," I said, "I don't drive and I've got flu at the moment. I don't know where his father is ... he was out with his father ... could you send him home in a taxi?"

"We will come round with him and see you, Madam," said the policeman. I dressed myself with shaky hands. Soon there was a knock at the door; I opened it to reveal Danny pinioned by two large men, a policeman on one side of him and a store detective on the other. The detective was also holding an enormous ball of white fluff. It looked like a giant powder puff. He handed it to me solemnly.

"Here is his anorak," he said. I peered down at it. Danny had shredded it so that the covering had disappeared and the lining had fluffed out. I knew that this was no laughing matter, Danny should not have taken the things from Woolworth's, but somehow the contrast between the solemn majesty of the law and the ball of fluff was so ludicrous that the whole thing seemed like a pantomime.

"Come in," I said. They came in nervously, clearing their throats. I realised then that these two men were terrified out of their wits. They had arrested Danny expecting the usual cowed delinquent, and Danny must have become like a raving madman. They just didn't know how to cope. I led them into the living-room while Danny stomped upstairs to his room.

"We should prosecute," said the policeman, shuffling his boots. "He was caught red-handed!" said the detective. They looked at me as if appealing for advice. I shrugged my shoulders.

"Danny is at this moment an inmate of Bethlem Hospital; he is there because of mental illness."

"Well, should he be allowed out, then?" asked the policeman.

"He has to be brought back into the world gradually," I put in. "It was the hospital's decision to send him home this weekend. We are only following their advice."

"Shouldn't he be better watched, then? The public should be protected."

I sighed. "The public aren't being heavily damaged. A few books isn't a high price to pay. Surely if people are fortunate enough not to have the problem of a child with mental illness, they can put up with a few inconveniences in the process of helping a sick person adjust to the world? I think I know why Danny did this. He was trying to prove something to Bethlem Hospital. Anyway, I'll pay for anything he took," I finished.

The two men looked embarrassed. "We took the things back that he stole," said the detective. "There's no damage except from the ashtray that he broke at the police station," said the policeman, "but we'll forget about that."

"He flung it across the room!" said the detective, his eyes wide.

When they had gone, I went upstairs to see Danny. He had taken a pair of scissors and cut off all his hair. It seemed almost Biblical the rending of garments and tearing of hair. I couldn't scold him. I sat on the bed with him and discussed what he had done.

He was very frightened at having been arrested.

Later when I saw Neill again at Bethlem, I discussed the incident with him. "You know, Danny's father was very angry at him for taking the things from Woolworth's, but I think Danny did it because he wanted to prove he was insane so he could stay at Bethlem."

Neill nodded. "I think so too."

I told him about the detective and the policeman and how frightened they were. Neill grinned. "Yep, mental illness affects people in strange ways!" he said.

"You know, I took a group of boys from here to Butlins Holiday Camp, and one of the little devils broke into a fruit machine and stole the money. They caught him and were going to arrest him, when I came and told them that he was from here. Then they wanted to let him keep the money! Can you imagine! He's hard enough to control as it is! I made the little bastard give back every penny he took."

Chapter Thirty-four

Delrow House

Danny was still at Bethlem Hospital when Jim and I were called to another conference about him. The doctors told us that Danny would have to leave there soon. We asked where he could go next; he was by no means normal yet.

The doctors suggested a place called Delrow House, a Rudolph Steiner centre for handicapped adolescents. They were prepared to take Danny as a day boy. The centre was mainly for Down's syndrome young people, but occasionally they would take in a disturbed adolescent of higher I.Q. They had found that the Down's syndrome young people were emotionally stable and could give emotional support to the disturbed ones.

We went to visit Delrow House. I liked the atmosphere, which was simple, artistic and homey. There were prayers before and after meals and a silent time in the evening for prayer.

Danny seemed to like the atmosphere and approve of the prayers, but his father couldn't agree to the change.

The next weekend that I came to see Danny I found him waiting dressed up in his suit with a suitcase and a heap of plastic bags around him. A nurse told me that I would have to take him home right away as they were discharging him. Then she disappeared.

It was a great shock. I had no money for taxis and wanted to ask if at least we could leave some things for my husband to collect by car, but the staff had all disappeared so there was no one I could talk to. I realised that they had done this deliberately, and felt deeply hurt.

Danny carried his suitcase and I carried all the plastic bags through public transport on a train, underground and train again. In my agitation I left the plastic bag with Danny's pills on the train going home, but it was discovered at the next station and brought back.

Jim was furious when he found how the Bethlem had just thrown Danny out. He thought it was because Danny had had his eighteenth birthday and the authorities were no longer responsible for his education. It seemed that from now on Danny would be dealt with as an adult.

Jim was determined to have it out with the officials at Bethlem. He asked for a meeting so that he could put his complaints. They agreed and we went in to see the doctors. Jim protested about the way Danny had been thrown out. They said that they had warned us that Danny would have to leave.

"We can't have him at home," Jim said. But they said nothing. Jim said that he was particularly worried as he was moving to a job in Scotland and would be away from the family a lot, and I would be left with the problem of Danny.

I was stunned. I hadn't heard before that Jim was going away. I felt a sick fear descending. It was bad enough with two of us trying to cope with Danny on my own it would be very difficult. Danny was very big and strong now. Yet unless he went to Delrow House there was no place for him to go but home.

I thought that at least we should try the offer that Delrow House had made to have Danny as a day boy, and when Danny was in a tractable frame of mind I suggested that he should write a letter asking to go.

Soon Danny received a reply to his letter, saying that he could start on the following week. The next problem was how he was going to get there. On the first day I went with him on the train, and from there the only way to Delrow House was by taxi. In the afternoon I made the same journey out to collect him.

I found him lying on the grass, talking to another boy. He frowned when he saw that I'd come to take him home, because it made him look foolish. "Tomorrow I'll go by myself," he said.

I agreed to this. Whatever the dangers of the journey, it would be better for Danny to feel independent.

On the next morning I sent him off with money for train and taxi, trying not to show my nervous fears. Danny went back and forth for a week. Then he began coming in later and later in the evening. When I asked where he had been, one evening,he blushed a deep pink. It turned out that he had walked to the station from Delrow and used the taxi money to gamble on some fruit machines in a nearby pub. I was inwardly amused at this escapade, but as he was so ashamed of himself, I decided not to encourage his tendency to gamble and looked as stern as I could manage.

By the end of another week, Danny was so shocked at himself for not being able to resist the gambling machines, and so tired by all the walking he was doing, that he asked if he could board at Delrow instead of going back and forth all the time.

Delrow agreed to take Danny as a boarder. They told us that Danny's behaviour had improved in the time he had been with them. He had stopped chewing and spitting out bits of paper, and he had begun to make friends and take part in the activities. They had a quiet time on Sunday evenings, when they lit a candle and sat in silence. I attended one evening and was struck by the lovely atmosphere. Danny was being softened by the gentleness and the spiritual quality of these people who had dedicated their lives to helping those around them in need.

Soon he was moved to a "family" house with a kind and understanding house mother called Eve-Marie. Danny became very fond of her. Now when he visited us at weekends, he insisted on saying grace before every meal as they did in Delrow.

Summer was approaching and we were told that Danny had been invited to go on holiday with a group from Delrow. They asked us to pack a small suitcase for Danny but begged us to keep belongings to a minimum. Danny and I had a fierce argument over the packing of the suitcase. He insisted on bringing his dressing-gown and slippers; nothing I said could dissuade him.

Later Betsy, the lady in charge of the trip, talked to me about it. "Oh, the trouble we had over those slippers of Danny's!" she said, throwing up her hands. "He kept losing them or forgetting them! Couldn't he have left them behind?"

I sighed, "Apparently he couldn't."

The next thing we heard was that Danny had a girlfriend! I first heard of her when Danny asked me to take a photo of her so he could put it in his wallet. Then he asked if he could bring her home for Sunday lunch. We went to fetch her from Delrow. She was called Ellen and was a pretty, very lively girl of Danny's age. She communicated very well in spite of being deaf and dumb and mentally retarded. Her movements were so expressive that you forgot that she couldn't speak.

As we drove to our house she kept pointing out of the car window at everything that amused her, and turning with a smile to show it to us.

When we arrived home Danny climbed out of the car, and began to look sulky.

Ellen ran over to him and studied his face. She put on a ludicrous imitation of his expression. He had to smile at that. Then she put up her hands and pushed Danny's feeble smile into a big grin. When he kept it there, she patted his face and gave him a kiss. There was nothing forced about his grin then.

Danny asked me to paint a portrait of Ellen for him, so after lunch I sat her down and did her portrait. She didn't sit very still so the portrait was very sketchy, but Ellen was fascinated by the result. I had thought that Danny wanted Ellen's portrait for himself, but he gave it to Ellen when it was finished.

My parents were a great comfort because Jim was away so much in Scotland. At Christmas time my parents went with me to see the Christmas celebrations at Delrow. They were very touched by the occasion. There was a huge tree with real candles and tangerines and home-made cookies hanging from it. Then there was a procession of the young people in white robes singing carols and carrying candles, their odd misshapen faces transformed into beauty as they sang. Danny too looked transformed, the anger and disturbance temporarily gone from his face, and an expression of peace illuminating it.

"How lovely this is!" my mother whispered to me. "So often you see people scorning or ignoring the handicapped, but here at Delrow they are valued and treated as important special people, which is what they are."

Chapter Thirty-five

Outings

During the next term at Delrow House, Danny seemed to be improving. He was doing eurhythmy, a kind of gymnastical dancing, he made toys in carpentry, and he worked in the garden.

From time to time I had to take him to the Maudsley Hospital to check if his drugs were correctly balanced. Danny did not like me collecting him from Delrow; he enjoyed making his own way to Euston Station, to meet me. However on one occasion he must have been going through a bad patch again, because when I got to Euston I was greeted by a Thing from Outer Space.

Danny had hacked off his hair in uneven chunks, as if a rat had gnawed it. He had rolled in the mud in the new jacket we had bought him for this occasion. The mud had caked in great lumps and cracked in a crazy-paving design all over his jacket, trousers and shoes, and he violently resisted my attempt to brush it off.

He slouched beside me silently as we made our way to the Maudsley Hospital, pausing to rummage through every dustbin we passed for old newspapers and magazines. After one attempt to stop him, I gave up. What was the point of worrying about appearances!

I was dressed up for the occasion, wearing a fur coat my aunt had passed on to me, so we looked a singularly ill-assorted pair.

However, I did have a sneaking sympathy for Danny's dustbin hunting. When I was a little girl in America, my friend and I loved going "garbage hunting" and would bring home wonderful treasures of old ribbons and shiny boxes. For Danny, the charm was that he could save money. He loved reading papers but hated spending money on them.

As he shambled along, I saw with sadness that Danny's beautiful straight carriage had gone. His head was bent and his back was stooped. He looked like a tramp, or the peasant in Millais's "The Man with the Hoe." I tried to push aside any feelings of false shame. What did it matter what people thought? All I had to do was get him to the hospital and back again.

At the hospital they were not overjoyed to see us. Danny left his mark where ever he went tracks of mud followed in his wake. At last the tests were finished, and with a sigh of relief I prepared to take him back. But now Danny turned a hopeful face to me and asked, "Aren't we going to have lunch somewhere?"

I couldn't quench that look, so we walked down the road looking for a cheap cafe where Danny's appearance wouldn't attract too much attention. Danny, however, chose an elegant place with flower boxes, lace curtains and real tablecloths. I argued with him but his heart was set on going in there.

I faced him squarely and informed him that he couldn't go in looking as he did. He would have to let me tidy him up. He consented, and I took stock of the situation. "Take off your jacket," I said, and was relieved to see that his sweater underneath was comparatively clean. Now for his hair: There were nail scissors in my bag; I sat him down on the curb and evened out his hair as well as I could. There wasn't much I could do about the trousers and shoes, but if I kept in front of him while we got through the door, we might pass muster. And if the restaurant found a little extra topsoil on their carpet at the end of the day, it could be used for the window boxes.

Danny cheered up considerably during the meal. He always loved good restaurants. By the end of the afternoon when we got back to Euston Station, he decided not to go straight back to Delrow. I put his muddy jacket back on him, feeling a bit sick at the thought of leaving him loose in Euston. Should I to try to escort him back to Delrow? He would hate that, and probably refuse to go.

As Danny was rooting around in the station dustbin looking for papers, a loud voice boomed in his ear, "Are you travelling, sir?" The words were spoken with elaborate contempt. Danny looked up and saw a large policeman glaring down at him.

I said, "He's travelling with me. He's my son." The policeman glanced from me in my furs to Danny, and then back to me, his eyes widening in disbelief.

Danny scurried to my side. "I think I'll go back to Delrow after all," he said quickly.

One day, just after his nineteenth birthday, Danny asked if we could visit Bethlem together. So we made the old journey for the last time, by train, underground, train and bus. Then we walked through the huge iron gates together, but this time I no longer felt the old dread. We went up to the ward where Danny had lived for so many years, and Danny looked around everywhere, seeing the new boys on the ward, and his old room with its new occupant.

Then he asked to see Neill, who came up to see Danny and shook his hand. Danny then presented him with a bottle of whisky. Neill nodded his thanks to Danny and Danny grinned back. You could see that there was a feeling of respect and friendship between them. As we left they shook hands again, and then we went out silently together. On the journey back I reflected that it had been a sort of Old Boys'

Reunion for Danny, but after this visit to Bethlem he never wanted to go there again. It was as if he had laid a ghost.

In the summer there had been a plan for Danny to go on holiday with his father, but when the time came Jim said he had to go back to Scotland and couldn't take him. "I'll take him another time," he said.

When Danny heard this he tramped upstairs without a word. Later I went up and saw him lying on his bed, with the bedspread over his face. He made no response to my questions.

I knew that Danny needed an adult male to take an interest in him. He was sick of being mothered. I telephoned my painter friend Richard Jones and asked him if he could drive Danny and me to somewhere interesting. Richard asked, "What does he like?"

"He likes Hitler at the moment," I confessed.

"There's a huge antiques market in Cambridge selling war memorabilia," said Richard. "They will probably have SS helmets and suchlike there. Would Danny like that?"

"I'm afraid so," I said, "and thanks very much!"

Richard came round and I went up to Danny's room and said, "We're going to a market that sells Hitler souvenirs." Danny's face emerged from the coverlet. "Where?" "In Cambridge. Richard's taking me, would you like to come?" Danny got up without a word and followed me downstairs. Then he stopped dead in his tracks. Richard was a dwarf.

This time, instead of shying away as he used to from anything abnormal, I felt a hidden empathy flowing from Danny to Richard. I sat in the back of the car, trying to make myself invisible. It was so good for Danny to make friends with Richard.

We had a lovely day; we went punting on the river, sight-seeing round the colleges and ended up at the antiques market. The best moment was when Richard donned an SS helmet and goose-stepped till Danny actually laughed. They both bought antique postcards and Richard purchased a German naval flag to use as a bedspread.

Finally we had a cream tea at Grantchester in the apple orchard. There were signs everywhere saying, "Please bring trays back" and "Please don't pick the apples."

Danny picked the apples and refused to take his tray back.

At the end of the afternoon, he spontaneously offered to buy us all ice cream. While he was gone, Richard said how much he liked Danny. "When you are small, people push you aside and knock you over. They don't do it deliberately, they just forget you are there. But Danny has been marvellous. He has been aware of me the whole time, and I can feel his compassion for me."

He added thoughtfully, "He treats you with a certain contempt, though, doesn't he?" I nodded. "It's his age, and I'm his mother."

"Yes," said Richard, "but it's very good that you were able to give him the security which enables him to sneer at you!"

"It's convoluted, Richard," I said, "but I think I know what you mean."

Richard drove us to different places during the holidays, and it made a big difference to Danny. Somehow the mutual concern that the two of them had for each other was a deeply healing experience.

I grew fond of Richard and invited him to join the Inscape Group, which was still flourishing. It was a great help as it gave me both friendships and encouragement in my art work. It was a little compensation for Jim's long absences.

I had hoped that somehow the separation would be helpful to our relationship; my parents had gone through many periods like this and my mother had always said it had been beneficial to their marriage, but sometimes, especially at night, I felt terribly alone.

Chapter Thirty-six

A Near-Death Experience

One weekend Danny came home very depressed, and nothing I did could cheer him up. He went back to Delrow, and on the following Thursday morning there was a phone call from Eve-Marie, Danny's house mother, to tell me that Danny had taken a large overdose of his own pills.

He was in the intensive care unit at Watford General Hospital, and his condition was critical.

A friend drove me to the hospital. Danny was lying on the white bed. He looked beautiful and at peace. Without the sadness that usually surrounded him like a grey veil, it was possible to see the beauty of his bone structure. His body had a kind of nobility of its own.

It was hard to believe that this strong young man was so ill and might die. I sat by his bed. He was in a deep coma. The doctors had a word with me and shook their heads. There was no guarantee that Danny would pull through or, if he did, that he would retain his intelligence. He might survive only to be a vegetable for the rest of his life. I went in to see him every day, but there was no change.

One day my sister Liz drove me in to see Danny, who was still unconscious after ten days. Liz told me not to give up hope.

"Things will change if he does recover," she promised. "This is an event. After a definite event like this, things are never the same. He may change his outlook. I have seen it happen before."

I knew that as a doctor, Liz knew a great deal, so her words comforted me. As I sat again by Danny's bedside, I thought hard about him. If he died, life would be easier for us all. Everything would go smoothly, the pressure on us would be over. But that smoothness and tidiness would be the tidiness of death. While Danny lived we had a share in the raw untidy world of suffering, we were part of it. It was very painful, but it was life.

Jim flew down from Scotland and went to see Danny in hospital. He sat by his bedside in silence. I had hoped that Jim would be a comfort but he was withdrawn and uncommunicative towards me.

On the following day when Jim and I went in, the nurses were excited. They said that they had felt Danny's hand move. One nurse said to me, "Take his hand and call him back." I sat by the bed and took Danny's hand. I tried to call his name, but no sound would come. How could I call him back to such a life?

When he heard that Danny would recover, Jim flew back to Scotland.

On the next day when I came in, Danny opened his eyes and smiled at me. I went home happy, and all that day the remembrance of Danny's smile was with me. On the following day a blizzard was raging, but I knew I had to go to see Danny, now that he had recovered consciousness. When I arrived, I found that he had been moved to the men's ward. I hurried over to his bed and when he saw me he smiled again! He opened his arms and we hugged each other. All his hostility and all my fears and hurt fell away. He was back to being my loving little son, as he was when he was a toddler.

He touched my coat wonderingly. There was snow on it.

"Snow?" he whispered. I nodded. Then he seemed to be making a great effort to tell me something. It was hard for him to speak; his throat was sore from all the breathing tubes that had been in it. Finally he croaked, "You know the books of C. Lewis ... of Narnia?" "You mean C. S. Lewis?"

"Yes, C. S. Lewis. I've been there. It was like another planet." His eyes roved wonderingly around the room. "Where is this?"

"This is a hospital," I told him. "You're in Watford." Then to forestall what might be his next question I added quickly, "You've been very ill, but you're getting better."

When I went in the next day he was sitting up, looking like Lazarus risen from the dead. The skin between his fingers looked decayed, and his face was like a skeleton's.

That evening the phone rang. It was the hospital. "Can you come in?" asked the nurse. "There's been an emergency." I telephoned my father and he drove me in. As I hurried along the corridor to the ward I saw a telephone with a figure sprawled over it. I leaned over to see if I could help. It was Danny; he had been trying to telephone me. When he saw me he raised a pathetic gaunt face.

"I want to come home," he said. "Can I come home?"

"Of course you can," I said, putting my arms around him to lift him up. We found the doctor in charge, who said Danny could go home if I would sign a paper discharging him. I gathered up Danny's few belongings and we staggered slowly down the long hallway together. He could not walk without support he was still too weak.

Just as we neared the end of the corridor he stopped and asked the question I had been dreading. "Why was I in hospital?" he demanded.

"You were sick," I faltered.

"What was wrong with me?"

"Can you remember?" I asked.

He stopped dead in his tracks and said, "I tried to kill myself." I nodded.

"I remember," he said slowly. "It felt as if I were drowning ..." We crept along together until we reached my father's car. He drove us home and I settled Danny for the night. He didn't eat much, but he insisted on having a bath, calling me nurse as I wrapped a bath towel round him and got him into his pyjamas. I tucked him up in his own little room again and said good night. It was a lovely feeling to have him at home as affectionate as he used to be. Then he told me again about the place he had been in that was like Narnia.

"It was beautiful, Mum. I wanted to stay there but they said I had to go back." He paused and thought for a moment. Then he said, "If I get better I want to help people—people like me."

I went to bed full of new hope, that maybe Danny had turned a corner and would be better from now on.

Late that night Danny knocked on my door and asked if he could stay with me. "It's the coldness and the loneliness," he said, shivering. He stood there like a child crying in the night to be taken into its mother's arms and comforted. Yet he was a man. I had a deep inner warning not to take him into my arms in bed as if he were a baby again.

I could not leave him comfortless either. I told him to lie on top of the bedclothes, then I got a quilt and covered him with it. Then I went back to bed, took his poor wasted hands and held them. All night long he clung on to my hands like a drowning man.

I was wrung with helpless pity. I told him we would go to Dr. Sutton as soon as we could, to see if he could help.

The next day was Christmas Eve; it was hard to get an appointment. We were told to come along and wait in the surgery at about three o'clock. We got a taxi to the doctor's surgery and waited a long time until at last Dr. Sutton could see us. He gave a startled glance at Danny's wasted appearance, and asked him how he felt. Danny lifted hollow eyes.

"It's just the coldness and the loneliness," he said.

A spasm of pity came over Dr. Sutton's face. He wrote out a prescription, and handed me a bottle of pills.

"Here are a few to keep you going. It'll be hard to find a chemist open now." At the reception desk I rang for a taxi to take us home, but there were none to be had at that time on Christmas Eve.

Danny became more and more cantankerous. He wanted to try to walk home but I knew he wasn't strong enough yet. Luckily a woman from our neighbourhood saw us and offered us a lift home.

I gave Danny the new pills which were to be taken in addition to his pills for epilepsy. They seemed to be effective, for he went out like a light and slept all through Christmas Day. On the day after Christmas I felt that Danny shouldn't be on such a strong dose so I cut the new pills in half, and Danny returned to a precarious normality.

The next morning I went down to clear up the kitchen. The housework had been badly neglected with all the problems on top of the usual Christmas mess. Danny came down in his dressing gown, looking very bad tempered. He grabbed a carving knife and threatened me with it, shouting that the kitchen was filthy and I was disgusting. I saw that his face had turned into that of a madman and a stranger.

I fell onto a kitchen chair and huge sobs forced themselves out of the depth of my being. I couldn't seem to stop.

Danny put down the knife with an anguished face. "I'll go to my room and stay there," he promised. "I'll keep out of your way."

That he should offer this to comfort me was unbearable. I gave him the full dose of pills again. He slept for the rest of the day, and the next day we went back to the doctor's surgery. After Danny had left the room I asked Dr. Sutton: "Is there any hope for him? Will he ever get better?"

Dr. Sutton shook his head. "I don't know," he said.

"Why must he have a life like this?"

Dr. Sutton shook his head again. "I wish I could answer that."

As the days went by it became clear that Danny's old depressive personality had come back in force. We were back to the same situation as before.

Chapter Thirty-seven

The Chalfont Centre for Epilepsy

Danny's unhappiness infected us all. He became withdrawn again, sitting in his room in the dark. He began to lose the ground he had gained in Bethlem and Delrow and I began to fear that he would become as bad as he was when he had his first breakdown. I asked Dr. Sutton whether anything could be done for him. He shook his head.

"The trouble is that he's depressed. Normally we can give 'happiness' pills that relieve the situation, but in your son's case the pills that he is taking for his epilepsy are given to depress his fits, so anything given to lift the depression would counteract the effect of those pills."

I saw that Danny was in a cleft stick. It was the same with his intelligence – it was precisely his intelligence that seemed to be his enemy. He could read people's minds. When friends came to the house, or if we met acquaintances outside, he could tell when they despised or feared him. He hated his ignominious situation and the menial tasks which were the only things he could do. Since his breakdown at fourteen years old his ability to concentrate had gone, and his cleverness was useless and destructive to him. I used to envy the mothers of the happy Down's syndrome children at Delrow.

One day when the thought of Danny's life became unbearably sad, the thought came to me: God loves Danny more than you do. This thought helped me to shift my attitude. If God had allowed Danny's existence, and if He loved him more than I did, then there must be a reason, a purpose for Danny's life, but I couldn't understand it or see it, and that question kept eating away at me. However, I began to try to let go my identification with my son, trying to trust God that things would work out for Danny's ultimate good.

Meanwhile, I could see that being at home was bad for him, but where could he go? Delrow House were not eager to take him back.

"The fact that he took an overdose proves that he was not happy here," said one of the organisers.

I went to see Eve-Marie, Danny's house mother. She was fond of him, and told me that Danny had once saved her life by getting someone to phone for an ambulance when he found her lying in the road, knocked down by a car. She agreed to intercede for him, and Delrow agreed to take Danny back for a short period while we looked around for another place for him.

Ann Harris, the Director of Delrow House, sent Danny the prayer of St. Francis:

O Lord, make me an instrument of your peace.
   Where there is hatred, let me sow love;
   where there is error, truth;
   where there is injury, pardon;
   where there is discord, unity;
   where there is doubt, faith;
   where there is despair, hope;
   where there is darkness, light.
O Divine Master, grant that I may not so much seek to be consoled as to console;
   to be understood, as to understand;
   to be loved, as to love;
For it is in giving that we receive;
   it is in pardoning that we are pardoned;
   it is in dying that we are born to Eternal Life.

Danny kept this prayer in his room, and when he went back to Delrow, he gave it to me as a present.

My sister Liz was very concerned about Danny. She was a consultant rheumatologist in a big London teaching hospital. Through her work she had come to know of a place for epileptics called the Chalfont Centre for Epilepsy. One day she came to see me, and told me about it. It was a lovely place with attractive buildings set in spacious grounds. Its senior physician was a Dr. John Laidlaw, who felt that people who had epilepsy should be treated with respect and allowed to keep their dignity.

Liz felt it might be just the place for Danny. It was also very near where we lived, only ten miles away.

"Now, there is something I need to know first: is Danny schizophrenic?" she asked. "They won't take psychiatric cases."

I repeated what the Bethlem Hospital had told us, that Danny was not schizophrenic, though his behaviour had been strange at times. Liz thought they might consider taking Danny. She helped us set up an interview with Dr. Laidlaw, and Jim, who was down for a visit, drove the three of us to Chalfont to meet him.

He was a handsome white-haired man with a distinguished face and a courtly manner. He questioned us both about Danny at some length, and was full of sympathy when I told him how Danny's pride had been hurt so many times by having fits and being stared at.

Then Danny was called in and Dr. Laidlaw spoke to him: "Well, young man, we would like to offer you a place here with us at Chalfont. We don't guarantee that you won't have fits, but at least here you can have your fits like a gentleman."

Danny glowed with pleasure at the man-to-man treatment he was getting. It sounded as if this place could give Danny the chance of a new start. We went home happier than we had been for a long time.

There was a list of clothes to buy, including a new suit for Sundays. I took Danny to a gentleman's outfitters in Halstead, and he tried on a new suit, complete with shirt and tie. He went over to the full-length mirror to see his reflection, and blushed with shyness. His head dropped down but he couldn't help stealing glances at himself in the mirror and trying to hide a big smile that kept breaking out.

He really did look different. The fact that he was wearing his new suit made him hold himself differently, and the thought that he had been accepted at Chalfont gave him a new purpose in life. He was to board there and come home for visits and occasional weekends.

All this time my parents had found it very difficult to help when Danny became mentally ill. Mother still had scars from her father's mental illness, and my father was very nervous of Danny's behaviour.

But they were wonderful with my other two sons. My father took a great interest in them and began to take the place of a father in their lives, as Jim was away so much. My father was particularly interested in their education. He was concerned when Charles failed his English and German O levels; although he was so brilliant at science, his languages were bad.

My father had sent his two sons to Oxford University and was very anxious that Charles should go there. He organised tutors for Charles so that he could get sufficient O levels to back up the A levels we hoped for in the sciences. Charles did get his language O levels with the help of the tutors, and after that it was plain sailing for him with his A levels, which were Physics, Chemistry and Mathematics. Charles decided to specialise in Physics. I was very impressed by the way he spoke of what he wanted to do.

"Mathematics is too unrelated to reality," he said, "and chemistry doesn't go deep enough. Physics deals with the laws governing reality. There is a growing realisation among scientists that physics is opening out into new areas which are more like religion than science. I want to be a physicist in the same way that Mother Teresa says she does her work. I want to do something beautiful for God."

My father spent a lot of time thinking of ways to further Charles's career, and wrote to my brother John, who was now one of the chief economists of New York City, and asked him to arrange for Charles to meet the Dean of Trinity College, where John had studied.

He did this, and Charlie made such a good impression that he was accepted on the condition that he obtained three A levels.

At last the exams were over and the notification arrived. I rushed upstairs with it, knowing that it was right that Charlie be the one to open the letter, but somehow on the stairs the letter got opened, and I read the news. Charlie had got a distinction in his three A levels. He had gained a scholarship to Trinity College, Oxford! I woke him with joyful shouts, and we stumbled down the stairs to celebrate.

Thomas, meanwhile, was achieving distinction as an athlete and bore home a series of trophies which adorned the mantelpiece. He tended to be cheeky in class, but when his teacher tried to keep him in after school, the football coach let him out, explaining to the irate teacher, "We need him for scoring."

Things seemed to be going well for my children and I was grateful but I missed Jim. I worried about our relationship because his letters were cold and distant and his visits were becoming less and less frequent.

Chapter Thirty-eight

The Occult

Now that he was happier in Chalfont, Danny began to develop his interests. He had become very interested in the "other world" since his experience when he was in a coma at Watford Hospital, when he felt he had been on another planet. Now he plunged into the world of the occult. Strange magazines began to arrive for him, and he sent away for protective amulets from the Tombs of the Ancient Pharaohs, and Sacred Talismans which had been a Rosicrucian Secret, kept till now.

He began to clank with all the medals and amulets he was wearing around his neck. He stuck prayers around his room. Some were very odd, like the prayer to the god of money, which you were supposed to repeat several times a day:

"I command thee, Avatar, in the name of Yah-va-ha-as to bring gold; and so to arrange my life that wealth may accrue. So mote it be."

In a few days a letter came from the Social Services to Danny with a cheque for fourteen pounds. Danny was convinced that this was the Avatar working. He began to plan what he would do with the huge fortune that he thought would be coming.

Another catalogue, "Potentials Unlimited," offered astral projection and mind-body healing and everything else right down to bust enlargement and increased self-confidence.

One group practised healing by prayer and love. It would have been touching if they hadn't demanded money all the time. Danny was always having to send off postal orders to them. They sent a prayer which he pinned on his door:

The Way to Happiness

Keep your heart free from hate, your mind from worry. Live simply. Expect little. Give much. Fill your life with love. Scatter sunshine. Do all you can for other people without thought of personal gain. Spread happiness. Try this for a week and *you will be surprised!*

This prayer came with a little piece of cloth that Danny was to wear all the time to bring healing.

One Sunday when Danny was on a visit home, we went to see Dorothy England together—Dorothy, my former pupil, who had kindly taken an interest in Danny years earlier. She had asked me to come with Danny on his visits to her as she was getting older and frailer, and Danny had had a fit at her house which had frightened her. We were having tea and a piece of Dorothy's excellent cake when Danny mentioned his interest in the occult.

Dorothy let him talk for a while, and then appeared to come to a decision.

She said, "Well, I'll tell you both something which I've kept a secret all these years. I am a spiritualist. I was in a circle in Watford, but it's been disbanded for twelve years. I don't usually talk about it to people because they think it's peculiar." She went on to describe her experiences while Danny listened wide-eyed.

Once in a seance a medium had told her that she was surrounded by helpful spirits, and as the medium was also an artist she could draw them. Dorothy fetched a roll of drawings from on top of her wardrobe and we saw the portraits of an Oxford don, an old Chinese doctor, a Red

Indian and a Spanish lady. She spread them out and said proudly that these were her particular spirits, who came to help her.

Then she fixed me with a powerful glance and said, "You are surrounded by spirits that help you paint. There's a Tibetan monk ..."

"Don't tell me any more!" I begged. Shivers were going down my spine. It was too uncanny. But Danny begged to hear more. Dorothy then told us about a seance she had been to, when ectoplasm had come out of the trance medium and formed a circle round the room. It was luminous and cloudy and the medium had played with it, throwing it around like wool, until it disappeared into his body again.

Then she had been introduced to the spirit of a Zulu chief, and out of nowhere a hand had materialised and shaken hers. It had been a hard, muscular hand, the hand of a warrior!

Danny was open-mouthed, his eyes popping out of his head with interest. Dorothy had acquired new glamour in his eyes. She went on to say that sometimes suffering is caused by bad behaviour in a previous life. Danny liked that explanation and mulled it over. He wondered if he had been Hitler in a previous life, and therefore his present life was a punishment for his past evil deeds.

We left Dorothy's house very stimulated, Danny clutching literature on spiritualism that Dorothy had given him.

When we arrived home I told Charles and Thomas about our visit. They were very interested. "Well!" I finished, "All I can say is, to quote Shakespeare, 'There are more things in heaven and earth than this world dreams of!'"

"If you're quoting Shakespeare," Thomas put in, "then it's, 'There are more things in heaven and earth, Horatio, than are dreamt of in your philosophy'!" I remembered then that Thomas was doing his English O levels.

That evening had been something that Danny and I shared, and he began to open up to me again. The next time he was home from Chalfont he began to talk to me spontaneously as we sat upstairs. He told me of the things that had hurt him when he was at Delrow. The thing that had wounded him the most was a remark of the eurhythmy teacher.

"She told me I stank!" he said, his eyes dark with the pain he had felt. I could well imagine that Danny didn't smell of roses, as I knew he didn't wash very often.

"I tried to kill her!" he said. "But they held me back."

I was horrified, but anxious to keep open this communication with Danny, so I didn't say anything.

"Do you like Chalfont?" I asked. Danny nodded. "There are two women on the staff I like—Nuala and Aileen. Maybe you could paint them." "All right, if you want me to," I promised.

Danny went on to describe the work he did in Chalfont. "We just pack cards," he said disparagingly. "It's stupid." I was thinking how to restore Danny's self-respect.

"Well, you know, you are very intelligent," I said, "that's why it's difficult for you." He nodded. Then, on impulse, I said, "You know, Danny, I've learned more from you than from either of the other boys."

I was rewarded by a beaming smile. And it was true, even if not quite in the way Danny thought. To turn his mind to better memories of Delrow, I remarked that Ellen had been such a sweet girl, it was a shame she had left. Danny gave me a shrewd look. "You know, I might not have liked Ellen so much if I hadn't been sick," he said. "I'm not sure I'd like her now."

One weekend Danny came home with a large box of incense. When I opened the door of the living-room, clouds of scented smoke drove me back. Danny sat in the middle of the clouds like some apparition from the last act of "Dr. Faustus."

A few weeks later he informed us that he was meditating. He wanted to make his room dark for this. He asked me to come and help. I drew the curtains and shut the door, but this wasn't good enough; the curtains were too light. I got some black material and hung that over the curtains. Danny pointed out that there were chinks on either side, so I taped the material flat against the wall. Then I went out, closing the door gently to let him get on with his meditating, but he called me back again. There was a chink of light coming from under the door!

By the time I had arranged the room to his satisfaction, what I was meditating on was nobody's business!

On the next visit Danny was into astral projection. I could see how he longed to leave his sick body and rove freely through the universe. He bought recordings that he persuaded me and his brothers to listen to; we sat together as a fruity voice with a Californian accent told us to sit back, relax and take a deep breath. Now we were ready for our astral journey.

The voice took us all over the place, to desert lands and to cities; then we were taken across to "the other side." First we journeyed through a kind of limbo where the land was peopled by pale ghosts. The next world after that, the Second Stage, was better. People were more real and were helping each other. The next world, the Third Stage, promised to be even more thrilling, but for that you had to pay another five pounds.

Danny began to arrive home with magazines that promised that you could cure yourself by thought. If you believed that you were better with enough faith, the magazine said, then you would become better. They even told epileptics that they need not go on taking their pills, once they had cured themselves by thought.

This made me really angry. I tried to point out to Danny the dangers of this way of thinking, but he had become an ardent believer. All his energy now seemed to be directed at curing himself by thought.

He did seem better each weekend and more positive. He told me that he had not had a fit for three weeks. I was very pleased for him and said so. Then he sprang his idea.

"I have been trying to cure myself so that I can live at home all the time," he said. "If I don't have a fit for three months, can I live at home?" My heart plummeted. So that was why he had been trying so hard! I felt all the pathos of it, and yet the thought of having Danny home all the time was a nightmare. It would be difficult for any of us to carry on a normal life.

I knew what would follow: Danny would retreat more and more into his room and become withdrawn again. I tried to explain this, to show him that he needed to live in a community, but all he could see was the bare fact that his mother did not want him to live at home.

Then the taxi hooted outside, it was time for Danny to go back to Chalfont. He gathered his few belongings together and went away with his head bowed.

I saw him get in the taxi, his head still bent. I felt like a murderer.

Chapter Thirty-nine

Thomas

Again on a Thursday morning the phone rang and a voice said in almost the same words as before, "Your son has had an accident, he has been taken to hospital."

"Has Danny taken another overdose?" I cried.

"Danny?" The voice sounded puzzled. "No, this is about your son Thomas. He was run over by a car this morning."

"Thomas!" I couldn't take it in. "It can't be! He's only just left for school this morning." "I'm afraid it is true," said the voice. "He was run over on his way to school." I felt my heart constrict Thomas, the happy-go-lucky one, in hospital. "How bad was the accident? Is he hurt?" I stammered, "Will he be all right?"

"He will be all right," the voice reassured me. "If you haven't got a car, would you like me to ask one of the parents to take you to the hospital?"

"Oh yes! Thank you."

I put the phone down and forced myself to think of getting on my coat and fetching my handbag. It was so hard to think that something could attack my other sons. I had come to think of them as invulnerable, because it was always Danny who was the sick one.

I hurried into the ward just as they were wheeling Thomas out of the x-ray room. The doctor showed me the x-ray: Thomas's thigh bone had been broken in two. It was a jagged break. He had been wearing his anorak with the hood up because it was raining, and he had just walked into the car without seeing it.

Thomas seemed in shock, but he could talk and he said he didn't feel any pain. He said, "Mum, when that car hit me I felt my life juggling in my hands for a moment. Then everything went black and I woke up lying in the road with the rain on my face, and people were bending over me asking if I was all right."

He was moved up to the men's ward, and I realised he was nearly fifteen years old and no longer a child. He was given a blood transfusion. A friend of mine, Sita, was a theatre sister; she said she would ask her favourite surgeon to look at Thomas. He came, and recommended a pin in the leg. This was a steel rod that they would place inside the bone to strengthen it until the bone healed, and then they would remove it.

Danny arrived for the weekend and we took him to see Thomas in hospital.

When Danny saw his active, popular brother lying in a hospital with his leg in traction, a broad grin of fellow-feeling spread over his face. From then on he lost his old envy and antagonism and began to treat Thomas as a friend.

The operation to put the pin in his leg was painful and Thomas suffered a good deal. On top of this his whole world of sport had been taken from him at one stroke. His coach came to visit him in hospital and told me that Thomas had been a promising athlete, even a brilliant one. "That very morning I was going to enroll him in a special training course to take part in athletics for the County."

The coach looked at me with moist eyes, "His triple jump was spectacular!" he said, shaking his head.

He told me that Thomas's career as an athlete was finished. A broken thigh bone, at the very time when intensive training should have taken place, meant that he could never now reach his potential. To my surprise and admiration, Thomas himself never complained; he just said that he was lucky to be alive.

When Thomas returned home, Danny's friendship with him continued and became a great support to me. Together we could even make Danny's visits home happy. But I didn't realise the price Thomas would have to pay for this new relationship with his brother.

Danny's depression was catching, and Tommy's sunny nature was put to the test. His accident had opened his eyes to the world of suffering, and he could no longer shut himself off from Danny's unhappiness. He seemed to wish to take some of that suffering on to himself. Unfortunately this meant that he was under great emotional strain. He began to wake at night with palpitations as I had done a long time ago. I took Thomas to Dr. Sutton, who became again the wonderful support that he had been when I first took Danny there.

Tommy derived great benefit from talking things over with Dr. Sutton. I saw that he and I were very alike. Probably he would have to work his way through his fears as I'd had to do. All that I could do was to be available to him and try to show him what I had found, that there was light at the end of the tunnel.

At this time he began to depend on me a lot, and I realised that I had probably neglected him in my earlier absorption with Danny.

One evening I was bending over Thomas, giving him his pills, and I saw his face light up with pleasure. Then I could see what it had been like in the past for him, back to his earliest memories, all filled with the sight of his mother always bending over the oldest child, giving him his pills, helping him after a fit, soothing him. I wanted to make it up to Tommy if I could. I had seen many times that in a child's adolescence a parent has a chance to repair some hurt or neglect in earlier childhood. Tommy himself felt guilty at claiming so much of my attention.

"I'm really sorry to worry you, Mum, and take up your time, when you have the trouble of Danny as well."

"Oh, Tommy!" I said, "If you knew the joy it is to be able to help someone! All those years I tried so hard to help Danny and I could do nothing."

Jim now came home to tell us that he had accepted a job in Libya with an oil company. He explained that because of Danny's problems he needed to earn enough money to help Danny throughout his life and so he had taken this job, although it meant that we would be seeing even less of him than before. I felt that I was being abandoned, but nothing I said could change his decision. As he said goodbye he thanked me for looking after the boys.

Chapter Forty

A Holiday With Danny

During the summer I planned to take Danny on holiday. Friends of ours had opened a hotel in Wales and we could travel there by train. Danny was twenty years old by now and he seemed to be more stable, so I thought I could take the risk of bringing him.

We enjoyed our ride up by train and had the luxury of a meal in the restaurant car together. Danny loved the ritual of a meal out; the reading of the menu, the table set out, the waiter bringing the food. He never seemed to mind what the meal actually tasted like, and could eat the most badly-cooked food without noticing, but he loved the ceremony.

To me, the meal on the train brought back memories of my older sister, Olga.

When we were children we were sent by ourselves on the train from Washington, D.C. to New York to visit our Grandma. As we travelled, Olga, who was eight and a whole year older than I was, said earnestly, as we peered out of the windows, "Make sure you enjoy this trip, Brigid, we'll remember it all our lives, won't we?"

So I did. And Olga seemed to be with me and Danny as the fields and forests flicked by the windows.

"If you could go anywhere in the world, Danny, where would you like to go?" I asked.

He considered. "I think I'd like to go to China or Russia." A scheme began to form itself in my mind. Perhaps

I could take Danny on a trip there for his twenty-first birthday. I had sold several paintings, so it would be possible; it would depend on how he behaved on this holiday. He seemed so much better.

We settled into the hotel without difficulty. Danny seemed to like his room, across the hall from mine. On the next morning after breakfast we explored the town. Unfortunately it turned out to be "unspoiled," which meant no shopping centres or arcades. I realised that Danny preferred spoiled places. He soon became bored. I racked my brains for something for him to do. We went on cliff walks together and had lunch out, and I booked a day trip to Skomer Island, a nature reserve. Danny looked forward to that.

On the day of the outing a man rowed us out to a tiny island and left us there. It was even more unspoiled.

There was nothing on it but cliffs and birds, nowhere even to buy a drink. I hadn't realised it would be as preserved as all that. Danny grew more and more bored and depressed. He kept wandering to the edge of the cliffs, especially to a place marked as a memorial to a little boy who had fallen to his death there. Danny went to stand at the very edge looking down, teetering back and forth.

I broke out into a sweat. Apart from my feelings for him, I could imagine vividly the gruesome mess and the difficulty of recovering the body if he flung himself over the edge. And then there would be all the bother with the press and police. ("What proof have we that you did not push him over the edge, Madam?")

I called to him, "Danny, come and tell me what this plant is—I think it's very unusual!" I called several times, pretending not to notice what he was doing.

At last he came over and said grumpily, "What is it?" I pointed to a weed nearby. "Do you think this is a rare flower?" I asked chattily, "I've never seen it before!"

"I don't know." Danny flashed me a suspicious look, but I went on chattering about botany, and after a while he followed me to the jetty. The dangerous moment had passed. We spent hours shivering on the landing. It was cold and the skies were a bleak grey. It started to rain and Danny began to eye the cliffs again speculatively, and move towards them, when at last the boatman appeared.

Danny climbed in silently, and stomped up to his room when we arrived back at the hotel. It soon became evident that he was back in one of his depressions. This made it difficult to have him in a hotel with other guests.

The fact that Danny looked more normal now that he was living at the Chalfont Centre brought its own difficulties, as people expected normal behaviour from him. Every conversation was loaded with mine fields. If people mentioned one of Danny's "King Charles's heads" such as anything to do with the occult or with ESP or with war ("Don't mention the war!"), he would begin to rave.

In the end I had to speak to them all privately to explain that Danny had "difficulties."

It was a huge relief when we got back and he returned to Chalfont. We spent Christmas with my parents as Jim was not coming home. Danny was still gloomy.

At Easter time Jim came back on a visit. He told me he had decided that he would take Danny on that long-promised holiday. He would make plans and let me know. "You have looked after him all this time," he said, "now it is my turn."

As Jim was leaving he heard that I was about to take Danny to Watford for an appointment with the optician, and said he thought Danny ought to go by himself. I saw Danny set out walk to the station, nervous and unhappy. Jim said goodbye to the rest of us and left for the airport.

Suddenly I knew what I must do, and I ran after Danny as fast as I could and arrived in time to catch him at the station. Danny was standing disconsolately on the platform. When he saw me his face lit up. "I'm coming with you," I said. Danny didn't speak until we were nearly there, then he said apologetically, "It's just that I'm afraid that I might have a fit!"

"I know," I said casually, "it's embarrassing for you and it's easier if there's someone else around." Danny nodded.

As we left the optician to go home, he said, to assert his independence, "I'm going home by myself!" and he disappeared into the distance.

On April 29th, his twenty-first birthday, I made a special festive birthday dinner, but it turned into an ordeal. Danny shut himself in his room and refused to come out. I thought sadly of all my plans to take Danny to China and Russia and now I couldn't even get him as far as the dining-room.

After a while I gave up and started serving the meal to Tommy and Charles, who was down from Oxford. Danny came and sat down glumly halfway through the meal. I brought in the cake and we sang "Happy Birthday" to Danny's scowling face. The only thing that cheered him up was one of my presents: an anti-religious book he'd asked for, by Nietzsche.

As the weeks progressed he became suicidal again. He had also taken to drinking wine. Alcohol was absolutely forbidden at Chalfont.

Most of the drugs used against epilepsy reacted badly with alcohol. But Danny had a reckless attitude to this and would walk around openly with his bottle of wine. I knew that Chalfont would not accept this, yet if Danny were dismissed I worried that Tommy, with his kind heart, would suffer. He was struggling with his own depression as well as with having to take his A levels this spring.

I wrote to Chalfont explaining that Thomas was already over-involved with Daniel and saying it would be very difficult at the moment if Danny were sent back home.

Chapter Forty-one

A Letter

The next weekend was difficult. Thomas was feeling the strain. His palpitations meant sleepless nights. I worried now about the friendship between Danny and Thomas and tried to think of ways of separating them, feeling at the same time a great sadness at the thought of taking Thomas's company from Danny, as it had become one of his few pleasures.

I knew also that it was only a matter of time before Danny was expelled from the Chalfont Centre. He had been breaking all the rules, and it was probably only because they knew the situation at home that they had allowed him to stay this long. Every time the telephone rang I felt a lurch in my stomach, thinking that this time it must be Chalfont telling me that Danny must leave.

Then one Saturday morning I received a letter. It was not from the Chalfont Centre but from Jim, asking for a divorce. I tried to hide my unhappiness from Thomas, and when Danny arrived I kept a cheerful face, but in the afternoon I became so depressed that I crawled into bed and covered up my head, trying to cope with this new blow.

There was a knock on my door. "Yes," I answered, "who is it?" Danny came in, dragging his feet, and slumped into a chair.

"Have you ever been depressed?" he asked me.

"Well, yes, as a matter of fact I have!" I retorted, rather more crisply than Danny expected. "Actually, I'm feeling depressed right now!" Danny stared at me bleakly—I had not given the sympathetic response he had been expecting.

After a while I relented. "I tell you what, Danny. I've heard that if you do something for someone else you feel better. So why don't we try that? You go down and put the kettle on for me and I'll come and make a cup of tea for you, and maybe we'll both feel better."

It must have worked because somehow we managed to get through that terrible day together.

I telephoned Dr. A. and asked if I could come and see him. I needed advice about what to do about Jim's letter. I needed help, too, in order to bear the pain.

Somehow I could not really believe that Jim wanted a divorce. In all the fairy tales, if a woman worked hard enough, if she wore out three pairs of shoes or performed three tasks with superhuman strength, then at last the man she loved would turn to her and love her again. I had endured so much, I thought that Jim would be grateful that I had gone on holding the fort. But this hadn't happened.

I clutched Jim's letter in my hand and walked up and down Halstead until it was time to see Dr. A. and his wife. When I knocked at the door they were both waiting for me. I had hardly sat down before I burst out: "Jim wants to divorce me!"

I looked at them both anxiously. In a way I was asking them whether this was too horrible to be borne or not; I felt on the verge of despair.

Dr. A. nodded his head to himself. It was as if he had heard something that he had been expecting. "Why don't you divorce him?" he asked. I was shocked. "But my marriage ... I want Jim!" I cried. They both looked at me piercingly.

"Why?" they asked. I was taken aback. Why? Why did I want Jim? He obviously didn't want me. Was it possible that I had been living in a fantasy, wanting a fantasy husband?

Dr. A. seemed to sense that I was in a turmoil. He spoke to me very gently.

"Look," he said, "it is hard for you at the moment, but on the other hand you have great riches inside." I felt that this was true; I felt rising in me the strength to bear this new trial. It was almost easier now that it was coming to a head. So many things had been going on underground before.

Dr. A. suggested that I write a letter to Jim saying that the feelings that I had for him when we married were still unchanged, and saying that I wanted to discuss the matter. I said that I would do that and got up reluctantly to say goodbye. I wanted to stay there with them and draw strength from them both, but instead I felt them withdrawing, just standing on their own ground, as it were, instead of leaning towards me in pity or sympathy which was what I had been expecting.

From their example I began to try also to contain my suffering, and not lean out to others for help too much.

When Jim next returned home I tried to hang on to this containment. I knew he hated any show of emotion. He arrived in the early morning and we were able to discuss things while the boys were still asleep. To my surprise, although his letter had been so cold, when we met face to face he agreed that we should try to keep the marriage going.

Then he wanted to see his sons. I went up to wake them to tell them their father was there. Thomas was sleeping deeply. Charles was down from Oxford and Danny was home on a visit as well, but none of them came racing down. After he had waited a while Jim said bitterly, "You would think that they would want to see their own father, especially after I've been away so long!"

"Well, you're hardly ever here. You don't share their lives anymore," I said sadly. He turned his head away.

Later as he was leaving again for Libya he promised that we could try to continue with the marriage if I wished.

On the following Thursday Dr. A. asked to see me before the meeting, and I went into the sitting-room where he and his wife were sitting. They asked me how everything had gone, and I told them what had happened.

"My husband has agreed that we needn't be divorced!" I finished, with relief. Dr. A.'s face lit up. "No!" he cried joyfully and I nodded. Mrs. A. gave me a glad look, but Mr. A. stood up, opened his arms and gave me a big hug. Up until now I had felt at a distance from them. I had been like a child, waiting to be scolded or praised, but now after this ordeal I felt I was in a new relationship with them both. I had begun to grow up!

A few weeks passed and then it was the last Thursday meeting before the holidays. I dreaded the thought of trying to manage without the help of the group, not knowing what crisis would happen over the summer.

Dr. A. invited me into his study as I was preparing to go, and asked me how things were at home. Danny had been very unhappy and difficult during his last visit, and his misery had weighed us all down.

"Why does his life have to be like this?" I burst out. "Surely there must be a purpose for it all somewhere?" Dr. A. didn't answer, and when I looked up I saw he had withdrawn deep inside himself and was sitting in silence. The silence was so profound that I was drawn into it; I sat still, and gradually in spite of my turmoil, a sense of peace began to steal over me.

After a while he looked up and gave me a loving smile of sympathy, then his eyes flickered with an inward look. He said, "Be courageous! I have a feeling that your life will change soon."

I was puzzled. How could my life change? It seemed that nothing could alter Danny's illness, or Jim's coldness.

But later I was to remember his words.

Part III

Life After Danny

Chapter Forty-two

Danny

One morning the telephone rang. It was a nurse from Chalfont who wanted to talk to me. She told me that Danny was suicidal. I said that Danny had been suicidal since he was fourteen; there was nothing anyone could do but take the best precautions one could for him.

I waited with sinking heart for her to say that now they were washing their hands of him and sending him back, but she didn't. After a pause she hung up.

That weekend Danny came home in a very bad mood. He talked all the time about cutting his wrists. I thought I detected a certain bravura in the way he was speaking, and felt a lot of what he was saying was said for effect. I tried to play it down and change the subject, and it seemed to work.

Danny was interested in geography and I suggested that he collect flags. I said I would write to John in New York to send an American flag, and Randal in Canada, and Olga in Africa could also send him one. Danny looked mildly interested and eventually Thomas and I got him listening to pop music and we went to bed.

At two a.m. there was a knock at my door. Danny was standing in the hall dripping with blood. He had sawed at his wrist with a razor.

I raced downstairs and dialled 999. An ambulance arrived almost before we had finished putting shoes and coats on. We were brought straight to the casualty department, where Danny was led away. At last they brought him back, his wrist neatly bandaged. We went home in a taxi, and then I made us both a cup of tea and gave us two aspirins each to calm our nerves. I saw Danny to his room and shuddered as my eyes fell on the bloodstained razor. I wrapped a tissue round it to throw it away. Danny saw me do it.

"Don't worry, Mum," he said cheerfully. "I wouldn't do it again. Not after the doctor has gone to all this trouble to sew me up."

I fell into bed and was just sinking into oblivion, when there was another knock at the door.

"Yes, Danny?" I spoke patiently, but through gritted teeth.

"Mum, could I have a photo of you in a frame? I want to put it by my bedside." I was touched in spite of myself. "Of course," I said, "only, do you think it could wait until morning?"

The next day Danny and I sat in the living-room and talked. "Please don't do that again, Danny," I begged.

"All right, I won't do it at home anymore," he promised. "Promise me you won't do it at all," I pleaded.

Danny didn't answer right away. He got up and paced the room. Then he turned and faced me. "You are afraid of death, aren't you?"

"Yes, I am," I replied.

"Well, I look on death as a friend. Sooner or later I am going to kill myself."

I felt caught in an iron vise. I realised that what he was saying was true. Yet how could I, his mother, accept it? I searched my mind for some words that I could say that might make a difference.

"But, Danny, I love you."

"I know you do," he said, "but you make me feel like a monkey on a string. I can't live my life for anyone but myself. And I don't want to live."

I still fought against accepting this terrible thing. "But I'll miss you," I said.

"I'll communicate with you through a spirit medium," he said.

He ended the conversation there, and from then on I knew that he was really going to kill himself. It was only a matter of time.

The thought came to me that I ought to warn Jim, otherwise he might not have a chance to see Danny before he died. I telephoned him to say that Danny was suicidal. Jim was annoyed at being telephoned; he said he couldn't believe it was that bad, but he came back in a few days and took Danny out to London. When they came home Jim said, "Danny was fine, there was nothing wrong with him. You're making a fuss about nothing."

Afterwards I asked Danny, "Did you tell your father that you were depressed?" "No," said Danny, "I didn't want to worry him."

Jim said he had now made all the arrangements for his holiday with Danny he was taking him to Ireland in July. I offered to come too, but Jim refused. He just wanted Danny. In any case, he said magnanimously, I had already done enough. Now it was his turn. It would be his chance to do something for Danny. They would tour all over and see different parts of the country, just father and son.

The evening before Jim was due to return to Libya, he told me that after all he had decided that a divorce was the only solution. He said he didn't care for me anymore. In the morning, helpless and miserable, I watched him go.

On Danny's next visit home he behaved badly. He arrived with a two-litre bottle of wine which he drank steadily, interspersing it with anything he could find on the shelf at home in the way of alcohol. He was too large to restrain forcibly, so I left him drinking downstairs and went to bed.

Next morning I came down early and found him still sitting in the kitchen. He had been up all night drinking. He still had a glassful of wine in his hand. I tried to plead with him to stop drinking and reached for the glass, but he was too quick for me. He flung it with all his force at the wall where it shattered, sprinkling the kitchen with glass splinters. I couldn't see any way of controlling him. The only thing I could think of was to send him back to Chalfont.

Luckily Charles had arrived back from Oxford the night before. I woke him and together, on Sunday, we drove Danny back to the Chalfont Centre. I got out with Danny and walked with him to the door. I wanted to say something loving but which would still show that I couldn't condone his bad behaviour.

"I'm sorry we had to bring you back, Danny, because you behaved so badly. I hope that you will ring up and apologise, and then we'll see you next week." He looked at me strangely. "Perhaps," he said.

I got back into the car. The thought came to me that I might never see Danny alive again, but still I couldn't see any other way that I could act, or anything else that I could say or do.

Chapter Forty-three

Death

On Monday morning the telephone rang. I picked it up and a voice said: "This is the Wexham Park Hospital. Your son was taken in this morning in a critical state. He has taken an overdose. He is in the intensive care unit. We will let you know if there are any developments."

I stared down at the floor. It fogged, then cleared again. I thought that I should send a telex to Jim. When I had done that I crouched by the phone, my head on my knees. I didn't know how to pray for Danny. I couldn't wish him back but I couldn't wish him dead either.

A little later the phone rang again. The same voice spoke: "This is the hospital. I am calling to let you know that your son died this morning."

I felt numb. And unreal. I rang my parents to tell them and asked them to drive me to the hospital. We drove together. Mother and I sat in the back and Mother held my hand. I felt cold and faint. I couldn't believe that Danny was really dead. We were shown into a waiting room and then a man came in and asked me to identify the body.

"The body!" I thought. Danny has become "the body"!

"I can't!" I said. "Can't my parents do this?" But it had to be a parent of Danny.

"We'll come with you," my parents said. That made it easier. Together we walked into the room.

I was touched and grateful that it had been made to look a bit like a chapel. There was an altar at the back and a candle on each side of a long bed, covered in a white sheet. I shivered, seeing the white sheet. The man there drew it back and my first impression was of nothing. There was nothing alive there. It was like an image made of clay. There was a shape like a face made of purpley-brown material. But where was Danny?

Fighting a sense of unreality I thought: I must identify him. Could it be Danny? I pulled myself together and focussed on the features. Those eyebrows, so like his father's. Thick, and almost meeting in the middle. Yes, it must be Danny. But he wasn't there!

The feeling of emptiness followed me home. I telephoned my sons and my friends; it helped me to realise that Danny had really died.

Charles came down immediately from Oxford, and was a great support. He drove me to Chalfont to collect Danny's things. Aileen, one of his favourite nurses at Chalfont, charged towards me with her head down and clasped me round the waist.

"Don't say a single word!" she begged. So we just hugged each other for a long time. She was right. There was nothing to say.

Later Charles, Thomas and I sat together over supper. Charles said, "You two look exhausted! I feel bad that I was at Oxford and couldn't be more help. It's been a long time since I felt any real contact with Danny. But I remember him best when we were little kids together."

"He really loved you then," I said.

I woke up that night. It was still dark, about three o'clock. I got out of bed and went to Danny's room. I sat on his bed and wondered if he were calling me, and if he were saying goodbye. I sat there for a long time, and then I went back to bed.

On the following morning Charles and I visited various undertakers, but they were completely booked. Then my father came to help us. He found some undertakers who would organise the funeral. Mother sent telegrams to my brothers in New York and Canada. They telephoned to say that they were coming to the funeral.

Jim arrived from Libya. He had been able to get away quickly because this was the day when he was leaving to go on holiday; to take the holiday with Danny that would never now take place. His face was drawn and he seemed shaken by Danny's death.

The funeral arrangements were completed, so Jim had nothing to do but visit the magistrate. This was for the inquest which would take place in a few weeks' time.

We had to go to a civic building where the judge, a dignified elderly man, sat at a desk in a room like a library. Jim and I sat side by side in two wooden chairs. The judge turned to me and said, "I believe you identified the body?"

I gave my account as well as I could, but something in the atmosphere of the place and the way the judge put his questions gave me a creepy feeling that I was in a murder case. Had I anything to gain from my son's death? Did I have access to him on the night it happened? It was then that I remembered.

"Danny promised that he would not try to kill himself at home anymore, and that's why he did it at Chalfont!" I was overcome to think that Danny had kept his promise.

After a while a reaction set in. I began to shiver. The judge kindly brought the questions to an end. He filled in a form and asked, "What shall I put him down as?"

"Well," I said, "he was epileptic and lived in a kind of home." Jim said urgently, "Couldn't he be put down as a student?" An understanding glance passed between the two men. "I'll write him down as a student," agreed the judge.

The next day was Friday, the day of Danny's funeral. As we entered the Church, my brother John pulled something from his pocket. It was an American flag.

"Look what I bought for Danny," he said. "I was just going to send it!" I was touched that he had thought of Danny.

"Just put it with the flowers," I suggested. I had been allowed to choose the readings for the service. My brothers were to be the readers. Randal read first, and finished with the verses that seemed to symbolise Danny's life:

"Fearfulness and trembling are come upon me, and horror hath overwhelmed me." And I said, "Oh that I had wings like a dove! for then would I fly away, and be at rest."

John read from Revelation: "And God shall wipe away all tears from their eyes, and there shall be no more death; neither sorrow, nor crying, neither shall there be any pain: for the former things are passed away."

It was a strange experience to be sitting there, knowing that this was Danny's funeral; that all that remained of him was in the box in front of us. I could see that Thomas could hardly bear to look at it. He sat on one side of me, and I could sense his inner turmoil. Jim sat on the other side of me. I felt him to be closer to me in spirit than he had been in years. The structure of the service seemed to uphold the order of the world against the disorder of death.

I kept feeling the powerful impact of death. It was a black nothingness. It was as if my life up until now had been a film, full of life and colour, and now it was cut off abruptly with Danny's death. Where there had been a life around

Danny there was nothing now. I was in a strange vacuum. All that I could feel was a big question: did I say yes or no to life?

Kneeling in church by Danny's coffin, I felt myself in the balance. I willed myself to say yes to life. When the service was over Jim took my arm and we walked down the aisle together, following the coffin. We drove to the cemetery outside the town, where the undertakers placed Danny's coffin by the newly dug grave.

Then an idiotic mistake took place. The undertakers found the American flag among the flowers. Two of them took the flag—the size of a tea-towel—and laid it reverently on the coffin. Placed there it looked just like a postage stamp, as if Danny were being posted to another world. The wind kept blowing it off as the prayers were being said, and the two moronic-looking undertakers would get up solemnly each time to replace it. They kept this up until the coffin was lowered into the grave and they couldn't reach it anymore.

I was suddenly overcome with hysterical laughter. John came over to me. "I didn't mean ... the flag!" He choked with laughter and we fell into each other's arms and laughed and cried together.

Then I saw a bus from Chalfont. Danny's friends from the Chalfont Centre had come to say goodbye. I went over and invited them back to the house. There Aileen and Nuala told us stories about Danny and his life at Chalfont. They and many of the young people there had been very fond of him.

Nuala said, "I think the flag was a very good idea."

"Oh, but it was a mistake!" I said, and explained how it had happened.

"Ah!" she said, "But it was so like Dan. He was different even at the end!"

"Dan did it when Nuala and I were both off-duty!" said Aileen with tears in her eyes. "He told me that he would kill himself, so I said that if he did, I would do the same and there'd be the two of us on top of each other. So he picked a time when we were both not there."

When Aileen and Nuala left, they begged me to come and visit and I promised that I would. At that moment to hear how fond all these people had been of Danny, in spite of all the difficulties he created and the problems of dealing with him, was no small comfort.

Chapter Forty-four

Another Funeral

It was strange now that Danny had gone. It was good to know that he was no longer suffering. I realised that his sadness had been in the background of my thoughts all the time. Now I knew he was at peace. I felt light-headed, like a balloon without its ballast.

I told my sister Liz about the queer lightness I felt, and she said that this was usual. She added, "You will have to go through a period of mourning."

Jim was relieved that I was so calm, and we seemed to be closer together again.

A few days after the funeral I had a phone call from Dorothy England. She had not been able to bring herself to go to the funeral but she told me that Danny had been in her thoughts constantly. She paused, and then said:

"I'm phoning you because I've had a message from Danny." I nearly jumped out of my skin. I had never told anyone about my conversation with Danny after he had cut his wrists, when he told me that after he died he would talk to me through a spiritualist.

Dorothy went on, "Danny said to tell you that he is all right. Because he died in an angry state, he needs to recover, so he is in a place of rest for three years before he will be allowed to move on. But he wants you to know that he is at peace now, and you must not be concerned about him."

I thanked her and put down the phone. I had already felt that Danny was at peace. Was there really a communication between that world and this one? I didn't know for sure, but I felt that what Dorothy had said about Danny was probably true.

On the other hand I had no wish to go into spiritualism too deeply. I knew I had a vivid imagination and could dream up all kinds of fantasies if I were not careful and imagine that they were true. I needed the path indicated by Dr. A., which brought me back all the time to reality and to the simple needs of the moment.

Some time ago I had arranged to teach painting for two weeks in Austria, while Thomas stayed with an Austrian family nearby. My parents thought I should go, they said that both Thomas and I needed a change. Jim seemed anxious that we should go, he said he was going to visit relatives in Ireland. I had hoped that the closeness between us would develop into a new chance for our marriage to work, but now I could feel that he was turning into a stranger again. So Thomas and I left for Austria.

We were met at Vienna airport by a friend and driven to Reichenau in the mountains. We were staying at a chalet-style hotel right underneath the lofty Alps. The first week of my teaching went well. I gave lessons in the morning and in the afternoons I would climb high up and paint the view. Up there by myself I could go through the period of mourning which, as my sister had predicted, now happened.

I had brought some photographs of Danny at different ages. I used one of these, taken when he was three, to put him in the foreground of my painting. Behind him rose the high mountains while a sky with golden clouds was glimpsed between them. I remembered how I had told him when he was little that God would come for him in a golden chariot. Had that fed his death wish? I thought of all the mistakes I had made and all the times I had let him down. Gradually I came to understand that because that was how I was then, things could not have happened in any other way. I let my guilty feelings go to rest just as I had learned to let Danny go.

After a few days, Thomas came to me. He was unhappy; he couldn't seem to raise himself out of his depression. I knew he had been burdened with too much emotional stress at too young an age. I saw his tension and remembered my own terrible time. Then a memory came of when I had gone to Dr. A. in just such a state and he had helped me.

I had been bent over with fatigue and fear, and Dr. A. had told me to ask my body to help me, not to allow it to give way to despair but to straighten my back. I repeated this to Tommy, who was slumped over in a chair. He sat up in surprise. I then told him Dr. A.'s words: "Say to yourself, I am not alone. There are other people working for the good of the world, together with me. Remember this: you are not alone."

I asked Thomas to sit straight and remember these words when he felt depressed, and said, "It is necessary to fight back against your fears."

Thomas stayed sitting upright for a long time, the light of battle in his eye.

A few days later I woke up very early in the morning. I climbed up the mountain and watched the sunrise over the mountains opposite. Then I thought of Dr. A. and said an urgent prayer for him. Suddenly some black crows flew by, cawing harshly. I felt a shiver go through me, like a premonition of something.

The next day I received a telegram. I was sitting at lunch. I opened it wonderingly and read the contents in disbelief. It was from my mother. Dr. A. had died. The funeral was the day after tomorrow.

I couldn't take it in. It was as if the bottom had dropped out of my life. I went upstairs, needing to be alone. A friend followed me, wanting to give comfort, but my need to be alone was so great that I found it difficult to speak to her. At last she left me. I sat down and tried to collect myself. Dr. A. had died. I had to accept this. I did not want to let him go. I felt like crying. I wanted to act out my anguish, but then I felt Dr. A. suddenly inside me, restraining me.

My grief for him must be worthy of what he was. Deep in me was what he had given me of himself. I must nourish and protect it so that he would not have given it for nothing.

When I told the seminar that I would be flying over to England for a funeral, they were sympathetic, trying to conceal their surprise that I would go and come back to finish the seminar as I had promised.

"The expense!" murmured the hotelkeeper. I said nothing. I had seen so often how money melts away, leaving nothing, whereas memories are very precious. I knew I had to go to the funeral.

Friends brought me to the airport, and from London airport I went to my father and mother's house. It was so peaceful to be there after the traumas at my own house.

Mother, Sheila and I went to the funeral. When I got out of the car I saw one of the members of the Thursday group. We embraced like children who have lost a father. It was strange to be at this funeral so soon after Danny's. There was a solemn moment when each of the men closest to Dr. A. put a spadeful of earth over his grave. It seemed to emphasise that his body had really gone. We could not look to him for advice or comfort anymore.

We were invited to the house afterwards. Mrs. A. and I embraced. She said, "We have had the same experience, you and I!" I felt a new link had been forged between us.

When I returned to Austria to finish my course, Thomas told me he needed to return home. He could not enjoy a new country while he was still in such a nervous state. I telephoned England. Jim was there and he said Thomas could come home and he would meet him at the airport. So I saw Thomas off, hoping that his father's support would be a comfort to him.

Chapter Forty-five

The Inquest

When I arrived back from Austria, Charles met me at the airport. He said Jim had gone to Ireland, and Thomas was with my parents. I was worried about Thomas so we drove straight to my parents' house, but when I saw Thomas I was reassured. He looked calm and happy and I saw that the affection and steadiness of my parents was just what he needed at this time.

Later I asked my mother what had happened. She said they had invited Jim and the two boys to Sunday lunch, but when they arrived Jim and Charles came in but Thomas stayed outside in the garden. Jim said it was best to leave him alone, as he was being difficult.

"Eventually," said my mother, "I couldn't stand it any longer, I had to find Tommy. I met him in the kitchen, just as he was coming in. His face was wet with tears.

"I just hugged him, and he said his father didn't understand that he had become so involved with Danny, and kept trying to make him pull himself together. But Tommy said he couldn't do it. 'I loved Danny,' he told me, 'he was my brother.'"

My mother's eyes filled with tears as she spoke. "I told him he was worn out and brought him upstairs and put him to bed. Then I went down and told Jim that he was acting like a bully! I said he was no better than Mr. Dombey who kept saying 'Pull yourself together' to his dying wife! To my surprise he took it all quite meekly. I said I would keep

Thomas here till you came back and he agreed to that. So he's been here ever since. We both love having him to stay."

I gave Mother a big hug. "Thank you for looking after him! If you only knew what he has been through! He was such a help with Danny!"

"It is marvellous for us that we can help at last," Mother said. "We could do so little for Danny."

When Jim arrived back he shrugged his shoulders when he heard that Thomas was still staying with my parents. "They'll just mollycoddle him," he said. "What he needs is to be toughened up."

The next day was the day of the inquest to investigate the cause of Danny's death. It was an ordeal. It was like a court case. Gran and I sat together, and Jim took a seat away from us.

A doctor from Chalfont gave evidence first. He said that Danny suffered from moderately severe epilepsy. They had tried some treatment for him in the form of new tablets but he did not like taking those, and pretended he was better.

"It was difficult to treat him," he said, "because whenever he wished to he could give the impression that he was well again. He was a very intelligent boy and he was able to make people believe what he wanted them to."

Another man reported how he had found Danny in an unconscious state on the morning of July 19th, a Monday.

Danny had taken the overdose on the Saturday night, so it was doubtful if they could have saved him. They got the breathing tubes into him and were carrying him into hospital when one of the ambulance men slipped and this militated against any effort to save him.

Then the coroner gave evidence. He said that the pills that Danny had taken were his own Tegretol tablets which he must have saved over a long period of time. When they were taken in too great a quantity there was no known antidote to those tablets, which contained carbamazapine. He described in detail the damage to the liver and other organs.

As he spoke, I stared at the radiator next me. This was the worst moment of my life. Nausea gripped me, and as each of my son's organs were discussed it seemed to me that he had been reduced to a thing, a collection of things. He had been torn apart in spirit, just as they were now tearing him apart physically. I could not get the images out of my mind.

Then the judge spoke. He asked me to confirm that I had identified the body as my son's. With a shock, I realised that I would have to stand up and give evidence.

My legs did not seem to be there. I looked up and tried to speak. The judge looked at me and then said that as I had already given evidence before, he could read my statement and I could just signal that it was correct.

His kindness at that moment gave me a feeling of space. I knew that there was something I had to say, but I was so confused that it was hard to know what it was. Then I realised: Chalfont had been very good to Danny, and his suicide there might damage their reputation. I wanted to put that right if I could.

The judge read my earlier statement, then asked me to say if it was correct. I said it was, then I turned to the Chalfont doctor and said, "Thank you for looking after Danny."

The doctor gave a start, then he looked touched and said, "That's all right."

At last the proceedings came to an end. They all agreed that it was clear that Danny had taken his own life. One psychiatrist said that he was surprised that Daniel had lived as long as he did, as he was severely depressive.

Now people got up and went out. Jim went out without looking back, but Gran and I linked arms, and wept together.

As soon as he could, Jim left again for Libya. Gran could see that our marriage was finished. "Maybe you should get a divorce," she suggested. I thought it over. Should I get a divorce now? Jim had asked for one some months ago, but something inside me had said, "Let it be. You are not strong enough yet."

Now people were very kind; a friend took me on holiday to Freiburg while Gran kept house for Thomas, who was still recovering.

After six months had passed since the funeral, Charles came down from Oxford on a visit and showed me a letter in which Jim had said that he was going to take a tough line with Thomas when he came back at Christmas. Then I knew what I had to do.

I wrote to Jim saying I now agreed to his decision to end our marriage. I would agree to a divorce on condition that he never tried to see me or contact me once the divorce was over. "Then I can pretend that you are dead like Danny," I wrote.

It was childish, but I knew I could bear it better if I could put our marriage in the grave with Danny, and then I could mourn for them both together.

When I had done that I felt so depressed I went to visit my sister Sheila. She told me to sit down and she sat next to me in silence. After a while I began to feel better and looked at her in surprise. She said, "I wanted to help you so much that I thought I would just sit here and try to give you energy, did you feel it?" I was surprised and touched, and told her how much better I felt.

Thomas managed somehow to work for his A levels, and sit them, though he was a bundle of nerves. I took him to see

Dr. Sutton, who was wonderful with him and tried various medications, but he warned Thomas that nervous illnesses take a long time to recover from, so he needed to be patient.

My family rallied round Tommy. Randal, who was now a professor in Canada with a wife and six children, wrote that he had gone through a depression during adolescence, and offered advice. Mother put him on a raw food diet, and Olga, my sister in Africa, heard that he was unhappy and asked if he would like to go to Africa and help run a summer camp for boys there. Thomas agreed to go, though he was still depressed and ill. I saw him off at the airport; he looked thin and pale, and my heart ached for him.

A month later I went to collect him, still fearful for his nervous state. I watched all the people coming out of the customs, worried that the trip might have added to Thomas's strained condition. I looked with envy on all the bronzed, handsome, self-confident young men that were emerging, and sent up a prayer that one day Thomas could be like that.

To my amazement I saw one of the group bounding over; he stood in front of me beaming with happiness, and said, "Hello, Mum!"

I was staggered. I never had a prayer answered more quickly!

Thomas bubbled over with his adventures. He'd been faced with a lion at the summer camp, he'd climbed Kilimanjaro with another boy and he'd made strong friendships. He and Olga had become fast friends, and he was already planning to return.

Meanwhile we had the good news that he'd passed his A levels with good marks and he'd been offered a place at Durham University, one of the oldest and most beautiful universities in England. Soon after his return Thomas set off, ready now for his new life.

After some time the divorce came through, and then I heard that Jim had married Alison. I thought I had let him go, but this news was like a fresh blow, and opened up old wounds. Once again I was filled with rage and jealousy. These feelings went round and round endlessly in my head. I tried all the ways to combat this, but my struggle seemed in vain.

Then one Sunday in Church we were saying the "Our Father" when these words hit me with great force: "Forgive us our trespasses as we forgive those that trespass against us." Alison had trespassed against me; how could I forgive her?

But did I want to be forgiven by God as I was forgiving her? I stopped and looked inside. There was no forgiveness there. There never could be. I felt that this hatred would never go away. What did Christ's words mean then? I had to try to forgive her.

In desperation I prayed and asked God to help me. I realised I was never going to be able to forgive Alison from myself, so I asked Him to forgive her in me.

Then I saw that for this to happen I would have to make a space—my hatred had filled me completely. So every time the thought of her came up, I tried to make a space. To keep the space clear I could not indulge in vengeful thoughts or speak of her nastily.

Miraculously, over a period of time, my hatred was taken away and I was given peace. From that peace I could even wish her and Jim well.

Gran and I still saw each other; Gran said, "You may have divorced Jim, but you're not divorcing me!" Her friendship became an important part of my life.

Luckily I had no money worries because my paintings were selling well. The Inscape Group had flourished and we exhibited all over the world now. Some of us were invited to exhibit in Germany at one of the greatest collections of Fantastic and Visionary art ever held. In the catalogue was a history of Fantastic art, starting from Hieronymus Bosch and Pieter Breugel, right up to Magritte, Dali and Ernst Fuchs of the Vienna School of Fantastic Realism. And following that, to my amazement, was a bit about the Inscape Group in England! My dream of long ago had been fulfilled at last!

On the following New Year's Eve, Mrs. A. gave a party for our Thursday group. She had become doubly precious to us now that Dr. A. had gone, and many of us felt that through her we were still in touch with him.

Mr. J., a new teacher, had joined the group and gave us fresh insights. I felt grateful for both of them because as my life had become easier, it was harder to remember my real aim. When I was suffering I was continually reminded to work on myself, but now I found myself becoming lazy and distracted. It showed me the dangers of a comfortable life, and I resolved to renew my commitment.

As midnight chimed Mrs. A. raised her glass: "I give you a toast to life!"

Just then one of the group entered the room with her three-week-old baby, who had been crying upstairs. It was a perfect moment.

Chapter Forty-six

Looking Back

While he was working on his doctorate in philosophy at Oxford, Charles came to visit one day to tell me of a strange experience he'd had. He was in a spiritualist church, and the medium looked in his direction and said, "Did anyone lose a relative lately?" Charles said that he had lost a brother. The medium said that this brother had been very unhappy in his life in this world, but he was now living through his brother's life.

Charles was very moved and said he had often felt a presence lately, as if Danny was sharing his life.

When I visited Dorothy England I told her about this. I saw her regularly after Danny's death, and we often spoke of him. Sometimes I agonised over whether I could have done things differently and whether this or that would have helped. Then Dorothy said, "I think you should stop worrying about it. There is a poem I often quote, by R. H. Grenville. It goes like this:

> Lot's wife brought to a glistening halt,
> Discovered a meaning sharp as salt.
> And I through the crystal film of tears,
> Regard once more the vanished years,
> Tasting the salty sting of pain,
> Hearing once more the sad refrain;
> Old as the ages, bitter and black
> Never look back
> Never look back.

"I think you are right in the main, Dorothy," I agreed, "but I'm going to look back just for a little longer. I'm going to visit the Chalfont Centre for Epilepsy. Nuala and Aileen have invited me to tea."

But before I visited Chalfont, I thought I would go once more to Delrow House to thank them for their efforts in the past for Danny. When I telephoned Ann Harris, the director of Delrow, she remembered Danny right away and invited me over.

Delrow House looked exactly the same; the old white building had the same friendly look, and the wood gleamed with polish. Ann received me in her office, a place filled with photos and cards from past and present co-workers. I asked after Danny's old house mother and learned that she was in a centre in Scotland, and very happy.

Ann had vivid memories of Danny. She felt that he had had great difficulty in forming relationships because of his illness and introversion. "Danny was so sensitive," she mused. "He saw too much. He was too aware in some ways. In Russia they call epilepsy 'the holy illness'. They feel that epileptics have a consciousness beyond the power of the body."

She shook her head, remembering. "Danny was such a gentle person. He had a troubled soul." She sighed, and I was struck by her concern for Danny still, after all this time.

"What led to your working here?" I asked. She smiled.

"It started forty years ago. I had been going to study art. Then I visited one of the Camphill schools in Aberdeen and was struck to my very being when I saw the children there, their distorted movements, their difficulty in speaking. That night I couldn't sleep. Inside me I kept hearing their voices and feeling their movements as if they were a part of me. From that moment I knew that this was a work I had to do.

"We opened Delrow House and immediately got referrals from the Maudsley Hospital from doctors who knew what we were trying to do. We try to create an atmosphere of positive love, to heal those who can be healed and to provide others with the freedom and space to take their own next step forward. One of the benefits is the way the people here help each other."

"Yes, Danny was helped a lot by Ellen," I agreed. I got up to go, reluctant to leave the peacefulness of Delrow which permeated the whole place. As I said goodbye, I was surprised and pleased when Ann told me that Jim had been sending them donations for several years.

A few days later I went to tea at Chalfont to meet Aileen and Nuala. They were very warm and welcoming. Several of the residents there reminded me of Danny, and it was like a little stab at my heart to see them. But the atmosphere was happy, a lot of joking going on the whole time.

They made the tea and we went into the staff room for a chat. It was empty except for a dog in the corner. They were full of reminiscences about Danny, saying he was a unique character.

"Do you remember all the phases he went through!" said Aileen.

"I remember his black magic phase—he'd have the Ouija board out—it gave me the shivers! When we stopped him taking the candles, he'd climb up and wrap towels round the ceiling light to make it dim.

"And then his smoking in bed! He was a shocking fire hazard! In the end we made a bargain with him, we said if he would promise not to smoke in bed we would let him use the staff-room at night. I'd get here in the morning and there'd be a thick cloud of smoke billowing out when I opened the door, and Dan in the middle of it! But he kept his promise he never smoked in bed again!"

"It wasn't only the smoke, it was the incense!" said Nuala. "I will never forget it! He burned it all night in the staff-room, and in the morning when I arrived I had to open a window and hang out of it, gasping and choking! You could tell him off, but it was like telling off a child. He'd look at you like a child, and you'd melt."

"It's funny how we all gave into him," mused Aileen. "We hated to hurt his feelings. Everybody loved him, that was the extraordinary thing! He never did a tap of work around the place, he never pulled his weight, but everybody loved him anyway."

"Yes," agreed Nuala, "yet if any of the others didn't do their jobs there'd be resentment and fights! People just accepted that Dan was different.

"I don't know why he was so popular, maybe it was because every now and then you could see his real personality coming through. When he smiled his whole face lit up. He was like a little boy then."

"But I think," said Aileen softly, "that it was when he was most normal that he suffered most. His intelligence was his worst enemy. If he'd have been a bit backward he'd have enjoyed the life here, but he was so intelligent he felt his life was wasted. Often I'd see him sitting on his bed, his head in his hands. He used to sit and think about what he was, and he couldn't bear it.

"He'd read the most extraordinary books. He'd give me them to read, and I'd have to admit that I couldn't understand them. You could never lie to Dan, he always knew when you were lying.

"He'd say, 'It's just that you aren't interested in the books, if you were interested you'd understand them.' One day he brought me the Watchtower magazine from the Jehovah Witnesses, and asked me if this was too hard for me to understand. I said, 'No, but I'm not interested.'

"I remember coming into the staff-room after a hard day with them all," she continued, "and saying, 'They'll drive me to drink, and there's no drink in the place!' Dan was sitting there reading one of his books on philosophy and I said, 'Dan, you're so intelligent and I haven't a brain in my head!' He looked up and said, 'You must be intelligent—you're able to handle all the people in here!' Dan never said much, but what he said was worth listening to."

"I remember the day of his birthday party," said Nuala. "We'd got him a cake and a little present. He was so moved, he couldn't speak and there were tears in his eyes. Everyone in the house had given him a present, even the ones who usually didn't bother themselves about anyone else. They gave him little things, or money. He just couldn't believe it. I said to him, 'You didn't think they loved you, did you?' He just smiled."

"He never believed that people liked him," sighed Aileen. "I think he was happy here but it only prolonged his life for a few years. He was suicidal and he was going to commit suicide sooner or later. The pull of the other world was too strong for him."

I got up to say goodbye and thanked then for all that they had done for Danny. They said it was nice to talk to Dan's mother. "He idolised you," said Nuala. "For him, his mother was his Queen." My eyes went a bit misty so I nearly stepped on the dog as I went out.

"That dog was sent here to Chalfont, he belongs here," said Aileen.

"You see," added Nuala, "he's epileptic."

Chapter Forty-seven

Conclusion

My parents celebrated their Golden Wedding in 1987. It was a joyous occasion, a kind of golden harvest. Around them were their children, their spouses and most of their seventeen grandchildren. They sat together, proud and happy at the head of the table, and one could see what they had gained by keeping together in spite of their great differences of character. They had led each other into a wider world.

My father had led a distinguished career as a diplomat and my mother was a recognised artist as well as a writer of twenty-five books. All their six children had achieved success in their chosen fields.

Thomas sat next me at the dinner and said, "You know, Mum, I think Charles and I weren't as affected by the divorce as we could have been because your parents became in a way our parents too. They were always there to help. Grandpa became a second father to us." At the end of the meal he and Charles proposed a toast to the happy couple.

Afterwards Liz's husband, Cliff, had a quiet talk with me. He must have guessed at the admixture of sadness in my joy at the occasion. He said, "Don't let your divorce spoil the past for you. Your husband did love you. I know, I was there. Events just became too much for you both. But you did have a good marriage at first. Keep the memory of those early years you had together." His words took away a little of the bitterness that I hadn't even realised was still there.

On the fifth anniversary of Danny's death, on a cloudy day in July, Charles, Thomas and I drove together to the graveyard. We brought some flowers to lay on Danny's grave. It was very quiet and there were no other people there. There were banks of flowers around the newer graves nearby. We three stood silently together. On the small plot in front of us, beneath our feet, were the remains of Danny's body, the body that had been such a torment to him. I thought of the efforts that had been made for him; had it all been wasted? Again the aching question returned: what was the meaning of Danny's life?

Suddenly as we stood there the sun emerged from a cloud and bathed the trees ahead in a golden light. And then in that moment I felt a great illumination inside me.

In a flash of understanding I saw that you can't find the meaning of anyone else's life. You can only find meaning in your own.

I thought of of all those years when I so wanted to know the purpose of Danny's life, and how it had started me on a search which had brought me so much in terms of understanding and growth. Through Danny I had met exceptional people: Dr. Sutton, Mrs. Watt, Neill in Bethlem, Ann Harris of Delrow, Nuala and Aileen in Chalfont, Miss Sandy, and through her Dr. and Mrs. A.

I thought of all the work, the caring for the sick, the mentally ill, the handicapped, that went on quietly without the world taking any notice. I had been forced, through Danny, to accept the side of the world that I had so much wanted to push away: the suffering and painful side.

I reflected on what I felt I had gained from Danny's life. I had acquired a broader horizon and been lifted out of my narrow self-enclosed world into something greater. In realising this, I saw that I was a part of everyone and everyone was a part of me. When I went into London and passed by the tramps sleeping under the Embankment bridge, I felt our common humanity. Every bent form huddled under piles of newspapers could have been Danny.

Some time ago a friend called Rita came to see me. Her son had died in a road accident. She could not accept his death. She wished she had been the one to die.

I knew so well how she felt; I had so often rebelled against Danny's fate.

But anger doesn't help. It can't heal, or restore a child. I tried to tell her that the best tribute to a child would be to recognise what one had gained as a result of having known him.

Rita thought this over, and then asked, "What helped you most?" I hesitated. "Well, there were three things, really. The first was my art. Exercising any talent you have can be a wonderful friend and support.

"The second and most important thing for me was finding a belief that sustained me through all that terrible time. I found my help through the Gurdjieff work but for another person the way forward might be entirely different.

"And finally what helped a lot was that I wasn't afraid of asking for advice from anyone!" I had to smile and added, "I must have been a damn nuisance sometimes, but as the Bible says, 'Ask and you shall receive.' So you have to ask!"

After she'd gone I kept thinking back to that very hard time with Danny. I saw that suffering has no value by itself but we can give it value by the way we accept it. It was like a fairy tale I had loved as a child, where the girl has to spin straw into gold. To do this she must first see the straw as potential gold, and then she must call on supernatural help.

So the sick or damaged child can be an opportunity for greater growth, wider understanding, deeper love.

And now as we three were gathered around the grave at this moment, it was possible to stand back a little from Danny's life and death and see them both in perspective.

I had set out on a path determined to find a meaning for Danny's life, and now at last I understood that it was his life that had given meaning to my own.

I looked at the two fine young men standing beside me, and thought what they had gained in compassion and understanding through what they had undergone in living with Danny.

Charles had grown into a thoughtful and sympathetic man, without the usual arrogance of the scientist, and Thomas had an eager interest in others and a wish to help them. We had all gained another dimension from sharing Danny's sad life. We could never now be unaware of the world's suffering.

As we stepped back from the grave, Tommy said softly, "We're glad we had Danny, aren't we!"

Epilogue

On Asperger's Syndrome
by Greg Scott

One of the great mysteries in life is human development, the process that happens in a child throughout its formative years and through adolescence. We know that this is affected by the environment, nutrition and immediate family, but there are also biological processes that limit this development.

I remember seeing a picture of Danny, it must have been about twelve years ago now, sitting on a rock against a non-descript sky, tall and thin, dressed like, well, like someone who didn't care much about clothes. There was something familiar in the man in the picture, the way he held himself, something that at the time I saw in the people I worked with.... Of course this could have been an association as at the time I was talking to Brigid about her story and about the son she had lost, a son she believed had Asperger's syndrome.

At the time I was working for a charity as a counsellor using cognitive behavioural therapy, and worked with a range of adults with Asperger's syndrome, pervasive developmental disorders, and high functioning autism. Most of the people I saw had been diagnosed late in life and many had been misdiagnosed several times along the way. All had significant problems with anxiety, and most experienced periods of deep depression. Most were independent. All had a sense of humour, a potential for enjoyment, and a degree of interest and empathy for people around them.

As is common in Asperger's syndrome, the majority of people I saw were men, and most of these described isolation and loneliness as significant problems in their lives, and all had suffered as adolescents, finding puberty and the years that followed difficult, confusing, isolating. A large number had attempted suicide.

It is nine years now since I worked with people with Asperger's syndrome and nine years since I saw the first draft of this book. I miss some of the people I worked with, and fear that some of them will have taken their lives as Danny did.

There is a need in my opinion for this book, both for its humanity and for its message of hope. The simple telling of two parallel stories, Danny's and Brigid's, set in a time and place but ultimately timeless, I believe will be of value to the next parent who becomes aware that their son or daughter has Asperger's syndrome. For though Danny died, there is a sense of the strength that we can find in discovering meaning through our suffering.

Brigid reminded me recently of something I said to her when we first met: "Just because someone has mental health problems doesn't mean they are any less entitled to consideration, empathy and compassion."

As a society we have a long way to go before this becomes accepted. This book will be part of that journey.

The following is an introduction to Asperger's syndrome:

In 1944 in Austria, Hans Asperger published a paper describing a group of adolescents whose behaviour shared similar patterns. Asperger described these features as "autistic psychopathy". Some of the features were similar to those described a year earlier in the U.S.A. by Leo Kanner as infantile autism. Features described by Asperger in his original paper included the following:

- Naïve, inappropriate social approaches to others
- Intense circumscribed interests in particular subjects, such as railway timetables
- Poor nonverbal communication
- Good grammar, but speech literal in content and odd in intonation
- monotonous, used for monologues not two-way conversations
- Poor motor coordination, often clumsy and uncoordinated in complex movements
- Level of ability in the borderline, average, or superior range, but often including specific learning difficulties in one or two subjects
- A marked lack of common sense
- Oddness in social relationships, lack of empathy
- Engagement in repetitive activities
- Dislike of disruption in routine
- Good rote memory but poor grasp of abstract ideas

Though Hans Asperger gave detailed descriptions of "autistic psychopathy," he did not offer specific diagnostic criteria. It is only since the 1980s that clear criteria have been developed and that autistic spectrum disorders have been classified as pervasive developmental disorders and not psychoses or forms of childhood schizophrenia.

All disorders in the autistic spectrum feature what has come to be known as the triad of impairments, namely impairments in social interaction, in communication, and in flexible imagination.

In typical childhood development, from early on in the child's life there is an inbuilt interest in the sight and sound of other human beings. Children with Asperger's syndrome often show a lack of interest bordering on indifference to others and may not appear to differentiate between people and objects in their environment.

From the second year on, children typically develop imagination and will begin to engage in imaginative and increasingly complex play and social interaction with other children. Imaginative play enables a child to pretend to be other people, and to take on their roles. Playing games of this kind depends on the child having developed the knowledge, inbuilt but taking time to emerge, that other people have different thoughts and feelings. This has been called "theory of mind": understanding that others have different mental and emotional states than one's own. As this emerges, pretend games help to improve the skills in understanding other people that are so necessary for integration into social life.

The person with Asperger's syndrome will typically have an uneven development across these areas of early development; though less debilitating than in autism, this uneven development has a ripple effect on other areas of the person's development.

As well as impairments in social development, there are difficulties that emerge in middle childhood that result from an impaired ability to make sense of information due to difficulty in filtering out relevant information from present and past information, i.e., memories and experience. This results in difficulties in predicting future events and in planning. This difficulty in filtering relevant information especially as regard to social situations can be a major disability, and also a source of acute anxiety.

There are also difficulties in the range of functions such as planning, flexibility, self-regulation and inhibition. These are necessary in order to plan goals for future activities.

People with Asperger's syndrome fall into three subgroups named after the way that the person interacts. These subgroups have been defined as Aloof, Passive, and Active but Odd (Wing).

The Aloof group is the least common in Asperger's syndrome. This group shows a combination of aloofness and passivity. In my experience this is predominantly a defensive response, and not an indication of lack of interest in people. Some people who fall into this group choose elective muteness as a way of interacting. Typically there is a sense of disconnection and an apparent lack of motivation. The presentation is deceptive and people can appear to have no emotional responses. It is only in the expression of strong emotions that one gets a sense of the person's verbal ability. This group can be highly dependent and require a lot of external support and prompting around areas of self care and daily life.

The Passive subgroup tend to be amiable, gentle, and are most likely to have passed through mainstream education. This group are more able to copy others' behaviours and respond positively to social approaches. This group are often painfully aware of their difficulties in social situations, but are able to function once they have established routines and often develop a high degree of independence. This group are the most socially motivated, though, and despite fearing rejection actively seek friendships and social relationships. This group have an understanding of social rules and norms, but these are often one-dimensional and do not adapt across a range of social contexts. This group experience social anxieties and in particular shame, with a fear of exposure and public humiliation. A common social strategy is compliance and a reluctance to express needs that could be summed up as "Don't ask, and you won't get rejected."

The Active but Odd group tend to be the most verbal and outwardly communicative of the subgroups, though their conversation tends to revolve around restricted topics of interest. This group are often socially naïve, and pursue interaction with others, but may have a tendency to stand too close or maintain eye contact beyond social norms. This group can have difficulty in learning activities outside their range of interests. This group can appear confident and in some cases grandiose, but this belies a fragility and vulnerability to criticism. When the person's interests are socially appropriate this group can be very social. However some people in this subgroup can develop anti-social traits, a situation that is worsened by this group's impulsivity.

References

Frith, U. (1991). *Autism and Asperger syndrome* (Cambridge University Press). Contains Asperger's original paper (1944).

Klin, A., Volkmar, F.R., and Sparrow, S.S. (2000). *Asperger syndrome* (Guilford Press).

Schopler, E., and Mesibov, G.B. (1992). *High-functioning individuals with autism* (Plenum Press).

Schopler, E., Mesibov, G.B., and Kunce, L.J. (1998). *Asperger syndrome or high-functioning autism?* (Plenum Press).

Wing, L. (1996). *The autistic spectrum* (Constable & Robinson).

Greg Scott, MSc., REBT
BABCP Accredited Counsellor,
Mindfulness Teacher

From the Epilogue by Greg Scott:

There is a need in my opinion for this book, both for its humanity and for its message of hope. The simple telling of two parallel stories, Danny's and Brigid's, set in a time and place but ultimately timeless, I believe will be of value to the next parent who becomes aware that their son or daughter has Asperger's syndrome. For...there is a sense of the strength that we can find in discovering meaning through our suffering.